Implementing a Winning Sales Department

From Zero

to Advanced

Revised Edition

Index

Who is this work for?

This work is recommended for entrepreneurs, business managers, and professionals who wish to create and/or improve a sales department in their organizations. It is also suitable for students and professionals in the sales field who want to delve deeper into strategies, techniques, and methods to improve their teams' performance and increase sales.

On the other hand, this work may not be suitable for people who have no interest in sales, team management, or entrepreneurship, as it specifically addresses these topics.

Introduction

Prepare yourself for a journey into the heart of the sales world. Straight to the point, no beating around the bush. The concepts in this work will change the way you think about sales.

This is not a book to sit on the shelf in your office. This knowledge should be passed on daily to everyone on the sales team.

Demanded, discussed, reassessed, and even questioned, as each company needs to develop its own sales culture.

Sales are the foundation of any successful business, and that is why building an efficient sales department is crucial for a company's long-term success. Whether you are starting from scratch or looking to improve your existing sales team, this book is for you.

"Implementing a Winning Sales Department: From Zero to Advanced" covers all aspects of creating a successful sales team. From hiring salespeople, training and development, setting goals, market analysis, sales strategies, to the role of marketing, customer service, and leadership in the success of the sales team.

The chapters in this book have been carefully selected to provide a comprehensive and practical guide to building an efficient and winning sales department, regardless of your company's size or industry.

With the help of this book, you will learn how to find the right candidates, set clear and achievable goals, create an effective sales pipeline, use technology to increase the efficiency of the sales team, handle customer objections, develop a sales culture in the company, and much more.

The methods and techniques presented in this book are based on years of experience and success in the market. The chapters were written by experts in sales and leadership of successful sales teams and are filled with practical examples and real-life cases.

Regardless of where you are on your business journey, this book will provide valuable insight and a practical guide to help you build a winning sales department and adapt to the constantly evolving market changes. Whether you are just starting out or already have an established sales team, "Implementing a Winning Sales Department: From Zero to Advanced" is the right book to help you achieve sales success.

The Importance of Building an Efficient Sales Department

The sales department is essential for the success of any company, regardless of its size or industry. It is through the sales team that companies generate revenue and acquire new customers, as well as maintain a healthy relationship with existing customers.

Therefore, it is essential to build an efficient sales department capable of meeting market demands and exceeding customer expectations.

To build an efficient sales department, some important steps must be followed. The first is hiring qualified and motivated salespeople with the appropriate profile to work in the company's industry.

It is important that candidates are selected carefully through a well-structured interview process, evaluating not only experience and technical skills but also personality, communication ability, and capacity to handle pressure and unforeseen events.

Another important step in building an efficient sales department is setting clear and achievable sales goals. These goals should be realistic and aligned with the company's strategic objectives and closely monitored by sales managers.

It is also essential that the sales team has access to tools and technologies that can help them achieve these goals, such as sales management software and CRM systems.

In addition, the sales team must be trained adequately and efficiently. Salespeople should be well-versed in the product or service they are selling, as well as efficient sales techniques like SPIN Selling and AIDA. Salespeople should also stay updated on market trends and innovations and develop interpersonal skills, such as empathy and emotional intelligence.

Leadership plays a crucial role in the success of the sales department. Sales managers should be inspiring leaders who know how to motivate the sales team and maintain a healthy and productive work environment.

It is also important for sales managers to be willing to listen and provide constructive feedback to the sales team so they can continually improve.

Another key aspect of building an efficient sales department is market analysis. It is essential for the company to understand its target audience and competitors well to develop efficient and differentiated sales strategies, develop buyer personas to identify customer needs and challenges, and address them efficiently.

It is crucial for the company to develop a sales culture that values the importance of the sales department for the company's success. The company should establish goals and objectives for the sales team and provide support and incentives for the team to achieve them.

Moreover, an efficient sales department allows the company to maintain its competitive position in the market. This is particularly important in highly competitive sectors where acquiring new customers and retaining existing ones is a critical success factor.

A successful sales department can also help the company expand its business, increasing market share and diversifying its customer base.

However, building an efficient sales department is not an easy task. It requires careful planning and a structured approach, from hiring talented salespeople to implementing well-defined sales processes and systems.

The following sections will present key concepts and practices that can help companies build an efficient sales department and achieve sales success.

One of the main pillars of building an efficient sales department is hiring talented salespeople. This involves identifying the skills and characteristics necessary for success in your company and then carefully evaluating candidates to identify those who possess these skills and traits.

It is important to remember that an efficient sales department largely depends on the quality of the salespeople in it.

Another crucial step is establishing well-defined processes and systems to support the sales team. This includes setting clear sales goals, defining success criteria for the sales team, and implementing a sales management system that can help manage and monitor the team's performance.

It is also important to provide continuous training and support to salespeople to help them refine their skills and acquire new knowledge.

In addition, market analysis is a critical element for the success of the sales department. It is important to understand the target market and competition to identify sales opportunities and develop effective sales strategies.

This involves creating buyer personas and segmenting the market based on key characteristics, such as behaviors, needs, and preferences.

Another fundamental aspect is creating an efficient sales pipeline and using lead qualification techniques to maximize the chances of sales success. This involves identifying potential customers and qualifying these leads based on well-defined criteria, such as buyer profile and available budget. It is also important to track and manage these leads throughout the sales cycle to ensure they are converted into sales.

Finally, it is important to remember that sales success is not just about techniques and processes, but also about people and relationships. An efficient sales department should be led by inspiring and motivating leaders who can create a strong sales culture and a cohesive team equipped with solid interpersonal skills, such as effective communication and teamwork, prioritizing the well-being of the company and achieving goals.

By following these steps and focusing on the key aspects mentioned above, companies can build an efficient sales department that contributes to their overall success. By continually adapting to changing market conditions, refining processes, and investing in the development of their sales team, organizations can achieve long-term growth and maintain a competitive edge in their industry.

Hiring Salespeople: How to Find the Right Candidates

Hiring salespeople is one of the most critical aspects of building an efficient sales department. After all, the success of a sales team largely depends on the skills and attitudes of its team members.

To find the right candidates, it is essential to begin by defining the skill and experience requirements for the position. This may include communication skills, negotiation abilities, technical knowledge of the product or service, sales experience, and so on.

However, it's not enough just to look for candidates with the right skills and experience. It's also crucial to find individuals who fit well within the company culture and sales team. After all, a positive and collaborative work environment can have a significant impact on productivity and team performance.

One of the most effective ways to find candidates is through referrals from other employees, customers, or business partners. Additionally, using job websites and social networks can be helpful in reaching a large number of candidates.

When interviewing candidates, it is essential to ask questions that allow you to assess their sales skills and experience, as well as their ability to adapt and learn quickly. It is also important to evaluate the candidate's attitudes and behaviors, such as their work ethic, confidence, and ability to work in a team.

Another approach that can be effective is conducting sales tests or sales simulations during the interview process. This allows you to evaluate the candidate's practical skills in a controlled environment.

However, hiring salespeople should not be a one-time process. It is crucial to invest in the ongoing development and training of the sales team, as well as establish a regular review process to assess team members' performance and provide constructive feedback.

In conclusion, hiring salespeople is an essential part of building an efficient sales department. By defining the skill and experience requirements, finding candidates who fit well within the company culture, and assessing their skills and attitudes through interviews and sales tests, it is possible to build a strong and successful sales team.

However, it is important to remember that hiring salespeople is only the beginning of the process of building an efficient sales department, and ongoing investment in team development is necessary to achieve sustainable long-term results.

The Importance of Professionalizing Hiring Processes

Selecting the right candidate for a sales position can be a costly and unpredictable process. It is necessary to find someone with the required technical skills for the role, as well as the personality and motivation to excel in the sales field.

Many companies choose to outsource their sales hiring process to specialized recruitment and selection agencies. While these agencies can be helpful in quickly filling open positions, they may not be the best option for companies that want to professionalize their hiring processes.

This is where the role of the human resources department or people managers comes into play in selecting new salespeople. HR professionals are responsible for evaluating candidates' skills and personality in a more comprehensive and strategic way, considering the company's values and desired characteristics in a candidate.

By having a specialized and well-structured HR department, the company can identify and select the ideal candidates for sales roles, and also have the opportunity to create talent recruitment strategies that can fill gaps within the department and the company as a whole.

Hiring the wrong salesperson can be expensive for the company. In addition to direct financial costs, such as recruitment agency fees, there are also the time and effort involved in training and integrating the new employee into the sales team. Moreover, hiring a salesperson who does not fit the company culture can negatively affect the entire sales team and even impact the company's reputation.

An effective HR department can help mitigate these risks. By professionalizing the sales hiring process, companies can ensure that they are selecting candidates who meet the desired technical competence and personality requirements. Furthermore, an HR department can develop an effective onboarding process to ensure the new employee is fully integrated into the sales team.

Hiring a salesperson is a critical process for the company. It is essential to keep in mind that the right hire can be a significant asset to the company, while a wrong hire can be extremely detrimental. Professionalizing hiring processes, through the recruitment of qualified and experienced HR professionals, can be a valuable solution to ensure that the company is hiring the best possible salespeople.

Suggestions for Sales Job Interview Questions

Here are some questions that can be asked during a sales job interview. It is up to the interviewer to choose which questions make the most sense based on the candidate's profile and the job opening.

1. How do you stay updated on the market and competitors?

2. How do you manage your time to achieve your sales goals?

3. How do you approach a potential customer who is undecided about making a purchase?

4. How do you handle customer objections?

5. How do you prepare for a meeting with a potential client?

6. Do you have experience with online sales?

7. Tell us about some experiences you had prospecting clients.

8. Do you prefer meeting your clients in person, by phone, or by video conference?

9. How do you approach consultative sales?

10. What is your lead qualification process?

11. How do you manage your customer portfolio?

12. How do you use social media to generate sales?

13. How do you handle rejection in sales?

14. How do you maintain motivation during challenging sales periods?

15. How do you build relationships with potential clients?

16. How do you manage follow-up with leads?

17. How would you handle an unhappy customer?

18. How do you communicate with different types of clients?

19. How do you prioritize your daily sales to-do list?

20. How do you measure success in sales?

21. How do you adapt to different clients' communication styles?

22. How do you use data to make sales decisions?

23. How do you handle pressure in sales?

24. How do you define success in sales?

25. How would you handle a situation where a customer cannot pay the full amount for the product?

26. How do you use negotiation techniques in sales?

27. How do you set and establish sales goals?

28. How do you approach building long-term relationships with clients?

29. How do you handle competition in sales?

30. How would you handle a customer with a technical issue with the product?

31. How do you use storytelling in sales?

32. How would you handle a customer who wants a customized solution?

33. How do you handle uncertainty in sales?

34. How do you develop an effective sales pipeline?

35. How do you define your pricing strategy?

36. How do you use marketing to generate sales leads?

37. How do you address customer needs and desires?

38. How do you handle a situation where a customer is not satisfied with the product?

39. How do you establish and maintain your sales networking contacts?

40. How do you use email marketing in sales?

41. How do you use gamification to increase sales productivity?

42. How do you adapt to different client personalities?

43. How do you handle change in sales?

44. How do you use SWOT analysis to evaluate sales opportunities?

45. How do you adapt to different business cultures?

46. How do you handle rejection in sales?

47. How do you use networking to generate sales leads?

48. How do you handle procrastination in sales?

49. How do you use humor in sales?

50. How do you manage client expectations?

Capturing Ideal Resumes

Advertising a sales position is a crucial step in attracting the best candidates and increasing the chances of successful hiring. To do this, it is essential to know the main channels of dissemination and how to use them properly.

Company website: One of the main ways to advertise a sales position is through the company's website. It is important that the job is clearly described, with information about the main responsibilities and requirements for the position.

Social networks: Another option is to use the company's social networks to advertise the job opening. You can create posts on major social networks such as LinkedIn, Facebook, Twitter, and Instagram, using hashtags related to the sales area.

Job portals: Job portals are excellent channels for advertising sales positions. Some examples include Catho, InfoJobs, Indeed, among others.

Employee referrals: Another way to advertise the job is through employee referrals. Employees can share the job posting on their social networks and refer people from their circle of relationships.

Headhunters: Headhunters are professionals specialized in finding talent for companies. They can help find qualified candidates who meet the job requirements.

When advertising a sales position, it is essential to use clear and objective language, highlighting the main requirements and benefits offered by the company. In addition, it is important to set a deadline for candidates to apply and establish an efficient selection process to ensure the hiring of the best professionals.

LinkedIn is highly relevant in the recruitment process for several reasons

Targeted audience: LinkedIn is a social network specifically designed for professionals, which means that the platform is an ideal place for businesses to find skilled salespeople and other professionals for their teams.

Advanced search filters: The platform allows recruiters and employers to search for specific candidates using advanced search filters, making it easier to find salespeople with specific skills, industry experience, or other relevant characteristics.

Advertising features: LinkedIn offers various features for recruiters and companies to advertise job openings, such as status updates and sponsored posts, which help businesses reach a large number of users on the platform and increase their chances of finding good salespeople.

Comprehensive candidate profiles: LinkedIn provides an environment where recruiters can assess candidate profiles more thoroughly than on other social networks or job platforms. Users can showcase their resumes, skills, experiences, peer recommendations, and more, allowing companies to evaluate candidates' skills and competencies in greater detail before inviting them for an interview.

Direct communication: The platform allows companies to contact candidates directly and initiate conversations, enabling more direct interaction with potential hires and potentially streamlining the recruitment process.

Overall, LinkedIn is an essential channel for finding good salespeople as it allows companies to find highly qualified candidates through advanced search filters, provides advertising features to maximize job posting reach, offers comprehensive information about candidates, and enables direct interaction between recruiters and candidates.

Defining success criteria for the sales department

Set clear and measurable objectives: The objectives should be aligned with the company's strategic goals and be specific, achievable, and time-bound.

Adopt modern and dynamic approaches: Use frameworks such as OKR (Objectives and Key Results) and KPIs (Key Performance Indicators) to set ambitious yet attainable goals and track progress.

Set individual goals for each salesperson: Establish challenging but realistic goals that take into account the individual's experience and skills. Offer an attractive commission plan to incentivize goal achievement.

Align success criteria with company culture: Ensure that the success criteria are in line with the company's values and mission. This will motivate and engage sales team members to work towards the department and company's objectives.

Monitor progress and adjust as needed: Regularly analyze success criteria and KPIs to identify areas of improvement and make adjustments as necessary. This will help maintain a high-performing sales department.By carefully planning and defining clear success criteria, a motivated and aligned sales team will contribute to positive results for the company.

How to train new sellers and ensure effective onboarding

To ensure effective onboarding for new salespeople and provide thorough training, it is crucial for companies to create an organized process that clarifies all doubts and caters to the specific needs of new hires. This will help them adapt to the work environment, systems, processes, and company culture. Here are some steps to follow for effective onboarding:

Provide a welcome manual: This should include basic information about the company, such as its history, values, mission, and vision, as well as details about the market and main competitors. The manual should be clear and concise, making new hires feel comfortable in the workplace.

Customize training: Training can be delivered through various methods, including in-person classes, online videos, and tutorials. It should be tailored to each new hire, considering their prior skills and knowledge, and focusing on specific areas they will need to master for efficient performance.

Emphasize company culture: The training should cover aspects such as communication styles, work practices, and values. It is important for new hires to understand the company culture from the beginning, making it easier for them to adapt and feel integrated with the rest of the team.

Teach systems and tools: New salespeople should learn to use the company's systems and tools, such as CRM and management software, from the start. This will enable them to perform their tasks efficiently and easily.

Assign a mentor: New salespeople should have an experienced colleague or mentor to help them adapt and answer their questions. The mentor should be a high-performing employee with experience in the company, sharing their knowledge and insights with the new hire.

View onboarding as a continuous process: Onboarding should not be seen as a one-time event but rather as an ongoing process that may last from a few weeks to a few months. Companies should continue to monitor new hires' performance, providing feedback and support as needed.

To ensure effective onboarding and success for new salespeople, create a customized training program that addresses each individual's specific needs, company culture, systems and tools usage, and integration with other employees. Continuously monitor their progress and provide feedback to ensure effectiveness and success within the company.

The Role of Leadership in Sales Department Success

A successful sales team is built on strong and motivating leadership. The leader's role is to create a positive and collaborative work environment, encourage the team to achieve challenging goals, and maintain a high level of engagement and motivation.

To be an effective leader in the sales department, it's necessary to possess certain key skills and traits. First and foremost, being a good communicator, listening well, and providing clear and objective feedback are essential. Additionally, having a strategic vision and setting clear objectives and goals for the team is crucial. Moreover, empathy and the ability to put oneself in the employees' shoes, understanding their needs and concerns, are important.

One of the main challenges for leadership in the sales department is keeping the team motivated and engaged. Adopting a transformational leadership approach, which seeks to inspire and motivate employees to give their best and reach their maximum potential, is crucial. This can be achieved through recognition and rewards, such as bonuses and commissions, as well as a positive and collaborative work environment.

Another way to motivate the team is through professional development and continuous training. Leaders should always look for new learning and development opportunities for their team, whether through formal training or mentoring and coaching.

During the onboarding process for new salespeople, it's vital that leadership is present and active. It's important that the new hire feels welcomed and supported from their first day on the job. The leader should introduce themselves, explain the company and team's expectations and objectives, and present the organizational culture and company values.

Throughout the adaptation period, the leader should provide constructive feedback and be available to answer questions and offer support. It's essential that the new hire understands the sales processes, the tools used by the team, and the strategies employed by the company.

An effective leader must possess communication skills, strategic vision, and empathy while adopting a transformational leadership approach that inspires and motivates the team. Professional development and continuous training are crucial for keeping the team engaged and motivated, and active leadership presence during the onboarding process is essential for ensuring a smooth and effective adaptation for the new hire.

How to set clear and achievable sales goals

Sales goals are the guide that directs the sales team to achieve the company's objectives, whether in the short, medium, or long term. However, setting clear and achievable sales goals is not an easy task. Sales leaders need to have a deep understanding of the business, the team, and the market in which they operate.

The importance of sales goals

Before delving into modern concepts of setting sales goals, it's important to understand why they are so crucial. Sales goals help the team visualize the path they should follow to achieve the company's objectives. They create a sense of direction, increase team motivation, and help monitor the performance of each team member.

Sales goals are also important for the company as a whole. They help control cash flow, predict future sales, and evaluate the sales team's performance. Additionally, sales goals can be used as a performance indicator for the sales department, allowing leaders to make strategic decisions based on concrete data.

Defining sales goals

Setting clear and achievable sales goals is a process that should involve the entire sales team and, of course, the leadership. Goals should be challenging enough to motivate the team but not so difficult that they become unattainable.

To set sales goals, it's important to understand the team's capabilities and the market in which they operate. This means analyzing past results, the team's productive capacity, the economic situation of the market, and the demand for the product or service offered.

It's also important to set individual and collective sales goals. Individual goals are important so that each team member has a sense of responsibility and knows exactly what is expected of them. Collective goals, on the other hand, help create a sense of teamwork and collaboration.

Modern methods of measuring results

In addition to setting sales goals, it's also necessary to measure results to see if the goals are being met. There are several modern methods of measuring results, such as OKRs (Objectives and Key Results), which are widely used in the business world.

OKRs are a simple and effective tool for measuring results and tracking team performance. They involve setting clear and quantifiable objectives, along with key performance indicators (KPIs). This way, it's possible to measure progress and make adjustments as needed.

Market Analysis: Understanding Your Target Audience and Competition

Understanding your target audience and competition is essential for making sales more effectively and with a higher chance of success. In this chapter, we will discuss in detail how to perform this analysis and the main aspects to consider.

First, it's important to define what the target audience is. This is the group of people or companies that have a similar profile and needs and are therefore more likely to be interested in the products or services you offer. To understand this audience, it's necessary to analyze their demographic, behavioral, and psychographic characteristics.

Demographic characteristics include data such as age, gender, income, education, and geographical location. Behavioral characteristics refer to consumption habits, purchase frequency, preferences, and brand loyalty. Psychographic characteristics are more subjective and involve aspects such as personality, values, and lifestyle.

By better understanding the target audience, it's possible to identify their needs and desires, as well as the main barriers preventing the purchase. Based on this information, more effective and personalized marketing strategies can be developed, increasing the chances of conversion.

Another important point in market analysis is competition. It's essential to know your competitors, their strengths and weaknesses, as well as their marketing and sales strategies. It's important to understand what they are doing differently, what they are offering, and how they are communicating with the target audience.

With this information in hand, it's possible to develop a differentiation strategy, with unique products and services that offer a perceived value greater than the competition. It's also possible to create pricing, promotion, and distribution strategies that are more effective and allow you to stand out from competitors.

In addition to understanding the target audience and competition, it's important to remember that there are fundamental differences in the approach to B2C (business to consumer) and B2B (business to business) customers. In B2C, communication should be more emotional and engaging, focusing on the benefits of the product or service to the customer. In B2B, communication should be more rational and objective, focusing on problem-solving and delivering value to the company.

Lastly, it's important to remember that the audience can be divided into warm and cold audiences. The warm audience consists of people who have already shown interest in your products or services, such as those who have registered on your website or contacted the company. The cold audience consists of people who are not yet familiar with your company or have not shown interest so far.

For the warm audience, it's essential to create lead nurturing strategies with personalized communications that encourage conversion. For the cold audience, it's necessary to invest in broader marketing actions that allow for greater reach and, consequently, interest from a larger number of opportunities.

The importance of applying the SWOT Matrix

Fonte: https://scopi.com.br/es/blog/analise-swot/

The SWOT matrix is a powerful tool that can be used in the process of developing and improving a winning sales department. This analytical tool, whose initials stand for Strengths, Weaknesses, Opportunities, and Threats, can help identify the sales team's strong and weak points, as well as the opportunities and threats present in the business environment.

Applying the SWOT matrix in the sales department begins with identifying the team's strengths. These strong points may include exceptional communication skills, industry experience, product knowledge, or solid relationships with existing customers. By recognizing and valuing these strengths, you can ensure they are fully leveraged and used as a foundation for success.

Weaknesses should also be identified and addressed. It may be that some team members struggle with handling objections, managing their time effectively, or adapting to new technologies. By identifying these areas for improvement, specific training and support can be provided to help team members overcome these barriers and become more effective in their roles.

Opportunities are external aspects that can be exploited to improve the sales department's performance. These opportunities may include new markets, changes in customer needs, or technological innovations. By identifying and seizing these opportunities, you can position your sales team for long-term success.

Threats are external factors that can harm the sales department's performance. These threats may include increasing competition, regulatory changes, or declining demand for a specific product. By identifying these threats and developing strategies to mitigate them, you can help protect the sales department and ensure its future viability.

By applying the SWOT matrix in the context of the sales department, you can gain a comprehensive understanding of the areas in which your team is successful and the areas that need improvement. This allows you to develop an effective action plan to drive success and create a truly winning sales department. Remember to revisit the SWOT matrix regularly, as the business environment and team needs evolve, thus ensuring continuous adaptation and improvement.

Keeping the SWOT matrix up to date and relevant is essential to ensure that your sales department remains agile and adaptable to market changes. To do this, it's important to establish a periodic review process for the matrix, involving all sales team members. This will ensure everyone is aligned and working towards the same goals.

Throughout the review process, encourage team members to share their insights and experiences. This will allow you to identify emerging trends, new opportunities, and potential threats that may not be immediately apparent. In addition, involving the team in the SWOT matrix review process also helps to increase motivation and commitment to the sales strategy.

When relevant changes in the SWOT matrix have been identified, it's crucial to adjust your action plan to address these changes. This may involve implementing new training, seeking new markets, or developing strategies to face increasing competition. By adapting your action plan based on the information gathered during the SWOT matrix review, you will ensure that your sales department continues to evolve and adapt to market changes.

Furthermore, it's essential to clearly communicate changes in the action plan to sales team members. Ensure that everyone understands the adjustments made and the impact of these changes on the team's overall goals and objectives. This will help ensure that all team members are working together and focused on the correct goals.

Applying the SWOT matrix to the sales department is a valuable way to identify strengths, weaknesses, opportunities, and threats. Regularly reviewing and adjusting the SWOT matrix and the associated action plan is crucial to ensure that your sales department adapts to market changes and continues to evolve. By involving the team in the review process and adjusting strategies based on the information gathered, you will create an environment conducive to success and excellence in sales.

Understanding the Sales Funnel

Fonte: https://blog.lahar.com.br/vendas/o-que-e-funil-de-vendas-etapas/

The sales funnel is one of the most important tools for any sales department. It is the visual representation of the sales process from the first contact with the potential customer to the moment of purchase. The goal of the sales funnel is to help the sales team understand at which stage of the sales process the customer is and what should be done to move on to the next step.

The sales funnel can be divided into four stages: attraction, interest, decision, and action. Each stage of the funnel represents a phase of the sales process. In the first stage, attraction, the goal is to attract as many potential customers to your business as possible. This can be done through digital marketing, advertising, or other customer attraction methods.

In the next stage, interest, the goal is to generate interest in the product or service offered by the company. This can be done through relevant content, sales presentations, and other persuasion tactics.

The third stage of the funnel is the decision, where the potential customer decides whether or not to do business with the company. In this phase, it is essential to present the company's differentiators, answer questions, and address objections.

The final stage of the funnel is action, where the customer makes the final decision and completes the purchase. It is essential to have an efficient sales closing process to not miss the opportunity to convert the customer into sales.

Each stage of the sales funnel is important and requires a different approach from the sales team. It is essential to have a clear strategy for each stage and know how to measure progress at each phase. This can be done through metrics such as conversion rates and sales cycle times.

To ensure that the sales team is aligned with the sales funnel, it is essential to train team members on how to use the tool and the best practices for each stage of the process. Additionally, it is vital for the sales team to have access to funnel data and metrics to make adjustments and improvements over time.

One of the main advantages of the sales funnel is that it helps the sales team identify bottlenecks in the sales process. This allows the company to make continuous improvements to optimize the process and increase the conversion rate.

The sales funnel is a key performance analysis tool for the team, helping the sales team understand the sales process, identify bottlenecks, and make continuous improvements to increase the conversion rate. It is essential to train the sales team on how to use the funnel and have a clear strategy for each stage of the process.

Sales personas development

Personas are one of the most important tools a sales department can use to better understand their target audience and create more effective sales strategies. They are detailed descriptions of your ideal audience - who they are, what their needs and desires are, and how they make purchasing decisions.

By developing accurate and detailed personas, salespeople can better understand potential customers and customize their sales strategies accordingly.

The process of developing personas begins with research. It is important to conduct interviews with existing and potential customers, as well as analyze market data, feedback on social networks, and other relevant sources. By doing so, salespeople can gather important information about their customers, such as age, gender, income, purchasing preferences, consumption behaviors, and more.

With this information in hand, salespeople can start developing detailed personas for different audience segments. For example, a company selling fitness clothing may have a persona for a 25-35-year-old woman who practices yoga, another for a 30-40-year-old man who practices weightlifting, and so on.

Each persona should be unique and personalized, with specific information about what the customer is looking for, their challenges and obstacles, and how they make purchasing decisions.

When developing personas, it is important to take into account the different sales channels. For example, the persona of a B2B customer may be very different from that of a B2C customer, and this can affect the way they prefer to be contacted and the message that resonates with them.

Once the personas are created, it is important to share them with the sales team and ensure that all members understand who these ideal customers are. This will help guide communication with customers, adapting it to their specific needs. Personas can also be used to segment contact lists and personalize marketing and sales campaigns.

In addition, personas are a valuable tool for assessing the performance of the sales department. By monitoring sales progress in relation to personas, salespeople can identify patterns and areas for improvement in their sales strategies. This can lead to real-time adjustments and optimization of the sales approach to better meet the needs of the target audience.

Developing personas is a fundamental part of the sales strategy of any winning sales department. By understanding their target audience more deeply and personally, salespeople can customize their sales approach and increase their chances of success.

Example to illustrate how this technique can be used in practice:

Persona: Anna

Position: Marketing Manager

Company: ABC Solutions

Industry: Technology

Age: 35 years

Gender: Female

Education level: Postgraduate in Marketing

Salary: 9,000/m

Marital status: Married, with a 5-year-old child

Interests: Reading, gastronomy, travel

Pains: Tight deadlines, difficulty keeping up with market trends

Goals: Increase the generation of qualified leads, improve the ROI of marketing campaigns

Product: Digital Marketing Automation Platform

Based on the persona Anna, it is possible to define more assertive marketing and sales strategies, such as presenting success stories of other technology industry companies that have managed to increase the generation of qualified leads and improve the ROI of marketing campaigns using the digital marketing automation platform.

In addition, it is possible to adapt the sales approach and communication tone according to the persona's interests and pains.

Creating and maintaining an effective sales pipeline

A sales pipeline is a visual representation of a company's sales process, from identifying leads to closing sales, that is, a map of the stages that make up the sales process. It is an essential tool for managing and monitoring the progress of sales opportunities and predicting future revenue.

Why is a sales pipeline important?

Having an effective sales pipeline is crucial for a company's success. It allows the sales team to track the progress of opportunities and quickly identify bottlenecks in the sales process. Additionally, it provides essential data for decision-making and revenue forecasting.

A sales pipeline also helps identify opportunities for improvement in the sales process. For example, if the sales team is struggling to convert leads into sales opportunities, the pipeline can help identify the stage of the sales process that needs improvement.

How to create an effective sales pipeline?

To create an effective sales pipeline, follow these steps:

Define the stages of the sales process. The first step in creating an effective sales pipeline is defining the stages of the sales process. Typically, these stages include:

a. Lead generation: This stage involves identifying potential customers who may be interested in the company's products or services.

b. Lead qualification: In this stage, leads are assessed to determine if they are suitable for becoming sales opportunities.

c. Opportunity identification: In this stage, qualified leads are identified as sales opportunities.

d. Proposal development: In this stage, business proposals are developed to present to potential customers.

e. Negotiation and closing: In this stage, proposals are negotiated and sales are finalized.

Define criteria for each stage

For the sales process stages to be effective, it is important to define clear criteria for each stage. For example, the criteria for the lead qualification stage may include company size, available budget, and need for the company's products or services.

Set goals and metrics

After defining the stages and criteria of the sales process, it is important to establish goals and metrics for each stage. This will allow the sales team to track progress and quickly identify bottlenecks in the sales process. For example, a goal for the opportunity identification stage might be the number of opportunities identified per month, while a metric for the negotiation and closing stage might be the average time needed to close a sale.

Use sales management software

To make the sales process more efficient, it is important to use sales management software to automate repetitive tasks, such as logging sales activities and tracking leads. The software can also provide detailed reports and analyses of pipeline performance.

Once the sales pipeline is created, it is essential to continuously monitor it to ensure it remains effective and functional. Here are some tips for maintaining an effective sales pipeline:

Update the pipeline regularly

Keeping the sales pipeline up-to-date is crucial for ensuring its effectiveness. The sales team should update the pipeline regularly, adding new leads, moving opportunities to the next stage of the sales process, and closing sales.

Use metrics to identify improvement opportunities

The metrics established in the sales process should be used to identify improvement opportunities in the sales pipeline. If a stage of the sales process is underperforming, the sales team should analyze the data to identify the problem and make adjustments to improve performance.

Analyze the pipeline regularly

Regular analysis of the sales pipeline is important to ensure it continues to function effectively. The sales team should analyze the pipeline regularly to identify trends, bottlenecks, and improvement opportunities.

Provide training for the sales team

The sales team should receive regular training to ensure they understand the sales process and know how to use the sales pipeline effectively. Training may include sales techniques, communication skills, and the use of sales management tools.

Adjust the sales pipeline as needed

The sales process and the sales pipeline should be adjusted as necessary to ensure they remain effective. If the company introduces new products or services, for example, the sales pipeline should be adjusted to accommodate these changes.

Communicate with the sales team

Regular communication with the sales team is essential for maintaining an effective sales pipeline. Discuss pipeline performance, address any challenges or concerns, and share best practices to ensure everyone is on the same page and working toward common goals.

Monitor and manage sales pipeline coverage

Sales pipeline coverage refers to the ratio of the total value of opportunities in the pipeline to the sales target. A healthy pipeline should have enough coverage to meet or exceed the sales target. Continuously monitor this coverage to ensure the sales team is generating sufficient opportunities to meet their goals.

Encourage collaboration among team members

Encourage sales team members to collaborate and share information about leads, opportunities, and successful strategies. This can help create a more cohesive team and lead to a more effective sales pipeline.

Regularly review and refine the sales process

Periodically review the sales process to identify areas where it can be improved or streamlined. This may involve updating the criteria for each stage, adjusting goals and metrics, or implementing new tools and technologies.

Celebrate successes and learn from failures

Recognize and celebrate the successes of the sales team, both individually and collectively. This can help boost morale and motivate team members to continue working toward their goals. At the same time, analyze failures and learn from them to make the sales pipeline even more effective in the future.

In conclusion, an effective sales pipeline is crucial for a company's success. By defining the stages of the sales process, establishing criteria for each stage, setting goals and metrics, using sales management software, and adjusting the pipeline as needed, the sales team can create and maintain a highly effective sales pipeline.

Regularly updating the pipeline, using metrics to identify improvement opportunities, analyzing the pipeline, providing training, and adjusting the pipeline as needed will ensure it remains effective and functional.

Methods for Qualifying Leads

By identifying and selecting leads with a higher likelihood of becoming customers, sales teams can focus their efforts and resources on the most promising opportunities, resulting in a more efficient and profitable sales process. In this chapter, we will explore various methods for qualifying leads, based on concepts and techniques established by leading sales books.

BANT Method

The BANT method (Budget, Authority, Need, and Timeframe) was developed by IBM and is one of the most well-known and widely used lead qualification methods. It is based on analyzing four main criteria:

Budget: Does the lead have a budget available to acquire the product or service offered?

Authority: Does the person you're speaking with have the authority to make decisions or influence the purchasing process?

Need: Does the lead have a real and clear need for the product or service offered?

Timeframe: When does the lead intend to make a decision and implement the solution?

Leads that meet all of these criteria have a higher likelihood of becoming customers and should be prioritized by the sales team.

CHAMP Method

The CHAMP method (Challenges, Authority, Money, Prioritization) was created in response to the limitations of the BANT method. It focuses on identifying the challenges faced by leads and evaluating their willingness to solve these problems. The CHAMP criteria are:

Challenges: What challenges does the lead face, and how can your solution help them overcome them?

Authority: Does the person you're speaking with have the authority to make decisions or influence the purchasing process?

Money: Does the lead have the financial resources to invest in the solution?

Prioritization: Is the solution you offer a priority for the lead at the moment?

This method helps sales teams focus on leads that are facing real problems and are willing to invest time and money to solve them.

GPCTBA/C&I Method

The GPCTBA/C&I method (Goals, Plans, Challenges, Timeline, Budget, Authority/Consequences & Implications) was developed by HubSpot and is especially useful for complex and long-term sales. It covers a series of criteria that help determine the lead's quality:

Goals: What are the lead's goals, and how can your solution help them achieve them?

Plans: Does the lead have plans to achieve their goals? How does your solution fit into those plans?

Challenges: What obstacles does the lead face to achieve their goals, and how can your solution help them overcome them?

Timeline: What is the deadline for the lead to achieve their goals and implement the solution?

Budget: Does the lead have the financial resources to invest in the solution?

Authority: Does the person you're speaking with have the authority to make decisions or influence the purchasing process?

Consequences: What are the consequences if the lead does not solve the challenges or achieve their goals?

Implications: What are the long-term implications for the lead if they choose your solution?

By analyzing these criteria, sales teams can gain a deeper understanding of the lead's needs, motivations, and concerns, allowing them to tailor their sales approach and increase their chances of success.

ANUM Method

The ANUM method (Authority, Need, Urgency, Money) is a simplified variation of BANT and focuses on four fundamental criteria:

Authority: Does the person you're speaking with have the authority to make decisions or influence the purchasing process?

Need: Does the lead have a real and clear need for the product or service offered?

Urgency: What is the level of urgency for the lead to solve their problem or meet their needs?

Money: Does the lead have the financial resources to invest in the solution?

This method is useful for quickly identifying qualified leads in fast-paced and results-focused sales environments.

FAINT Method

The FAINT (Funds, Authority, Interest, Need, and Timing) method is another variation of BANT designed to adapt to changes in the modern sales process. The criteria for FAINT are:

Funds: Does the lead have financial resources or access to resources to invest in the solution?

Authority: Does the person you are talking to have the authority to make decisions or influence the buying process?

Interest: Does the lead demonstrate genuine interest in the offered solution?

Need: Does the lead have a real and clear need for the product or service offered?

Timing: What is the ideal time to approach the lead with your solution?

By using the FAINT method, sales teams can adjust their approaches to better align with the expectations and realities of the current sales process.

Lead qualification is an essential part of a winning sales department. By using effective lead qualification methods, such as BANT, CHAMP, GPCTBA/C&I, ANUM, and FAINT, sales teams can identify and prioritize opportunities with a higher probability of success, optimizing their resources and improving their results. The key is to choose the most appropriate method for your business, adapting it as necessary, and training your team to apply it efficiently and effectively.

Strategies to increase lead conversion into sales

Converting leads into sales is the ultimate goal of any sales department. To achieve this goal, it is essential to implement effective strategies that can increase conversion rates and drive business growth. In this chapter, we will explore various proven strategies to increase lead conversion into sales.

Build solid relationships

Establishing solid and lasting relationships with leads is critical to increasing conversion rates. Trust and empathy are key factors that influence the buying decision. Therefore, sales teams should strive to understand the needs and challenges of leads, offering personalized solutions and added value.

Focus on benefits, not features

When presenting a product or service, it is crucial to highlight the benefits and value it provides, rather than just focusing on the features. Leads are more interested in how your solution can solve their problems and meet their needs. Therefore, by communicating benefits, sales teams are more likely to convert leads into customers.

Implement a structured sales process

A well-structured and standardized sales process helps ensure that all opportunities are handled consistently and efficiently. In addition, a structured process allows sales teams to identify bottlenecks and areas for improvement, continuously optimizing their approaches and increasing conversion rates.

Efficient follow-up

Follow-up is a crucial part of the sales process. Contacting leads at strategic times and in a personalized manner can make the difference between closing a sale or losing an opportunity. Sales teams should use CRM and sales automation tools to streamline the follow-up process and ensure no leads are forgotten.

Continuous training and development

To maximize conversion rates, it is essential to invest in continuous training and development of the sales team. This includes improving communication, negotiation, and closing skills, as well as staying up-to-date on market trends and changes. Well-trained and informed teams are better equipped to handle objections and convert leads into sales.

Establish a sense of urgency

Creating a sense of urgency can be an effective strategy to motivate leads to make a purchase decision more quickly. This can be done by offering limited-time discounts, highlighting product scarcity, or emphasizing the opportunity costs of not acting immediately.

Overcome objections

Objections are a natural part of the sales process and should be treated as opportunities to clarify doubts and provide additional information. Sales teams should be prepared to handle common objections and develop strategies to overcome them. This includes demonstrating empathy, actively listening, and providing clear and convincing answers that address lead concerns.

Leverage testimonials and case studies

Testimonials from satisfied customers and successful case studies are powerful tools that can help increase lead conversion into sales. They provide social proof of the value and effectiveness of your solution, helping to build trust and credibility. Be sure to share relevant testimonials and case studies with your leads during the sales process.

Personalize your sales approaches

Each lead is unique and requires a personalized approach to increase the chances of conversion. Sales teams should strive to understand the specific needs, preferences, and motivations of each lead, adapting their sales tactics accordingly. This may include segmenting leads based on specific criteria, such as company size, industry, or geographic location, and creating personalized messages and offers for each segment.

Setting goals and monitoring performance

Setting clear and measurable goals is essential to drive sales success. Sales teams should set realistic conversion goals and regularly monitor performance, identifying areas for improvement and adjusting strategies as necessary. Additionally, it's important to celebrate and reward success, encouraging ongoing motivation and commitment from the team.

Increasing lead conversion to sales is essential for the success of any sales department. Implementing effective strategies such as building strong relationships, focusing on benefits, implementing a structured sales process, efficient lead tracking, investing in training and development, creating a sense of urgency, overcoming objections, utilizing testimonials and case studies, personalizing sales approaches, and setting goals and monitoring performance can help maximize conversion rates and drive business growth.

Success in lead conversion to sales requires ongoing dedication, adaptability, and commitment from sales teams and organizational leadership.

Negotiation techniques for salespeople

Negotiation is an essential skill for successful salespeople. Mastering negotiation techniques can help close sales efficiently and ensure satisfactory results for both parties involved. In this chapter, we will explore several proven negotiation techniques for salespeople based on validated sales concepts and strategies extracted from leading sales authors.

Prepare for negotiation

Preparation is the key to a successful negotiation. Before entering a negotiation, salespeople should research and understand the lead's needs, challenges, and objectives, as well as their own limits and goals. This includes knowing the features and benefits of the product or service they are selling and being prepared to answer questions and objections.

Build rapport and trust

Building rapport and trust with the lead is essential for effective negotiation. This can be achieved by demonstrating empathy, listening attentively, respecting the lead's time and opinions, and being honest and transparent throughout the negotiation process.

Be assertive, but flexible

Successful salespeople are assertive in defending their interests and those of their company, but they are also willing to be flexible and find mutually beneficial solutions. This may involve making concessions in some areas to gain advantages in others or presenting creative options that meet the needs of both parties.

Reciprocity principle

Reciprocity is a powerful psychological principle that can be used to your advantage in negotiation. By offering something of value to the lead, such as a discount, a free consultation, or useful information, you create a sense of indebtedness that can lead to concessions on the lead's part.

Use the power of silence

Silence can be an effective negotiation tool, especially when used after making a proposal or presenting a counterproposal. Silence creates tension and can cause the lead to reconsider their position or make a concession. Additionally, listening attentively and giving space for the lead to speak allows salespeople to obtain valuable information that can be used during the negotiation.

Control your emotions

Maintaining emotional control during negotiation is crucial for success. Salespeople should avoid showing frustration, anger, or impatience as it can damage rapport and trust. Instead, adopt a calm and rational approach, focusing on the facts and benefits of the proposed solution.

Use anchoring

Anchoring is a negotiation technique that involves establishing a reference point or "anchor" from which negotiations can proceed. This can be done by presenting an initial proposal that is favorable to you but leaving room for negotiation. By establishing an anchor, you influence the lead's perception of the value of the offer and can facilitate the attainment of a more favorable outcome.

Learn to handle objections

Facing objections is a common part of the negotiation process. Successful salespeople know how to effectively handle objections by addressing the lead's concerns and providing additional information or alternative solutions. When facing objections, it is important to listen attentively, show empathy, and respond with clear and well-founded arguments.

Make concessions wisely

Concessions are an inevitable part of negotiation, but it is crucial to make them wisely and strategically. When making concessions, make sure they are proportional to the concessions made by the lead and do not compromise your ultimate goals. Additionally, when making a concession, try to get something in return, reinforcing the principle of reciprocity.

Know when and how to close the deal

Closing the deal is the final stage of negotiation and requires specific skills and tactics. Successful salespeople know how to recognize when a lead is ready to close and use effective closing techniques, such as assuming the sale, offering a last-minute incentive, or asking a closed-ended question that directs the lead to make a decision.

Mastering negotiation techniques is essential for salespeople looking to close sales efficiently and ensure satisfactory results for all parties involved. By properly preparing, establishing rapport and trust, being assertive and flexible, using principles such as reciprocity and anchoring, controlling emotions, addressing objections, making concessions wisely, and closing the deal, salespeople can maximize their success in negotiations and boost overall sales performance. Practice and experience are crucial to refining negotiation skills, and salespeople should always be willing to learn and adapt to the specific situations and challenges they face.

How to Handle Customer Objections

Dealing with objections is an inevitable part of the sales process. Customer objections can arise for various reasons, such as concerns about price, uncertainty about the effectiveness of the product or service, or a lack of understanding of the customer's needs. Knowing how to handle objections effectively is essential for converting leads into sales and ensuring the success of your sales department. Here we will explore proven strategies for handling objections.

Listen carefully

The first step in dealing with objections is to listen carefully to the customer. This demonstrates respect and empathy and helps to identify the root of the objection. Ask questions to clarify the customer's concern and make sure you fully understand the objection before responding.

Stay calm and be patient

Staying calm and patient when dealing with objections is crucial for success. Avoid becoming defensive or aggressive, as this can harm the trust and rapport with the customer. Instead, maintain a positive and professional attitude when addressing objections.

Validate the objection

Validating the customer's objection means acknowledging and showing understanding of their concerns. This can be done using phrases such as "I understand your concerns" or "It's a legitimate issue." Validating the customer's objection helps to establish rapport and demonstrate empathy.

Address the objection with facts and information

When responding to objections, present clear and convincing facts and information that directly address the customer's concerns. For example, if the customer is concerned about the price, explain the added value your product or service offers and how it justifies the cost. If the objection is related to the effectiveness of the product, present case studies or testimonials from satisfied customers that prove the results.

Use targeted questions

Asking targeted questions can help address objections and lead the customer to reconsider their position. For example, ask the customer what is causing hesitation or what would be needed to alleviate their concerns. This can help identify specific areas that can be addressed to overcome the objection.

Offer alternative solutions

In some cases, it may be helpful to offer alternative solutions that address the customer's concerns without compromising your own sales goals. This may include offering a flexible payment plan, a free trial period, or the possibility of customizing the product or service to meet the customer's specific needs.

Practice the "feel, felt, found" technique

The "feel, felt, found" technique is an effective strategy for handling objections and involves three steps: acknowledging the customer's feeling (feel), empathizing by sharing that other customers have felt the same way (felt), and then presenting how those customers found satisfaction or solution by using your product or service (found). This technique creates a sense of understanding and community between you and the customer and offers a positive response to the objection.

Know when to retreat

Although it is important to address objections and seek solutions, it is also crucial to recognize when to retreat. If the customer remains inflexible after several attempts to address their concerns, it may be more productive to politely end the discussion and reach out again at a more appropriate time.

Track and learn from objections

Tracking customer objections and analyzing your performance in addressing them can provide valuable insights to improve your sales skills and refine your approach. Use this information to identify patterns and areas for improvement, as well as to train and develop your sales team.

Practice and refine your objection-handling skills

Handling objections is a skill that can be refined through practice and experience. Invest time in personal training and development, as well as in improving the skills of your sales team. This includes attending workshops, reading successful sales books, and practicing objection-response techniques in sales simulations.

Handling customer objections is an essential part of the sales process and requires effective skills and strategies. By listening attentively, remaining calm and patient, validating objections, addressing concerns with facts and information, asking targeted questions, offering alternative solutions, using the "feel, felt, found" technique, knowing when to retreat, tracking and learning from objections, and continuously practicing their skills, salespeople can overcome objections and efficiently and effectively convert leads into sales. Practice and experience are key to mastering the art of handling objections, and salespeople should always be willing to learn and adapt to specific situations **and challenges they face.**

The Importance of Follow-Up in Sales

Follow-up is a crucial step in the sales process and plays a fundamental role in building long-lasting relationships with customers and generating successful sales. Often, salespeople underestimate the importance of follow-up, which can result in the loss of valuable opportunities.

Why is follow-up important?

Follow-up is important for several reasons:

Strengthens the customer relationship: Follow-up allows you to demonstrate genuine interest in the customer and their needs, which helps build rapport and trust.

Increases customer satisfaction: Following up ensures that the customer is satisfied with their purchase and that any issues or concerns are addressed promptly.

Generates additional sales: Effective follow-up can lead to additional sales, whether through upselling, cross-selling, or referrals.

Improves customer retention: Satisfied customers are more likely to do repeat business and become loyal customers.

Provides feedback opportunities: Follow-up provides an opportunity to collect valuable feedback about your products or services and identify areas for improvement.

Timing and frequency of follow-up

Timing and frequency of follow-up are critical to its success. It is important to contact the customer soon after the sale or initial interaction, but without being overly intrusive. A good starting point is to follow up within 24 to 48 hours after the sale or initial interaction. After that, the frequency of follow-up should be adjusted based on the type of customer and the nature of the business relationship.

Follow-up methods

There are various ways to follow up with customers, and it is important to choose the most appropriate method for each situation. Some of the most common methods include email, phone, text messages, social media, and in-person visits. Each method has its own advantages and disadvantages, and the choice of the correct method will depend on the customer's preferences, the nature of the relationship, and the message you want to convey.

Content of follow-up

The content of follow-up should be relevant, personalized, and value-driven. Avoid generic messages and focus on addressing the customer's specific needs. Some tips for creating effective follow-up content include:

Thanking the customer for their purchase or interaction

Providing useful information or relevant updates to the customer

Addressing any concerns or questions the customer may have

Offering additional support or assistance if needed

Presenting upselling or cross-selling opportunities in a helpful and appropriate manner

The importance of CRM (Customer Relationship Management)

Using a CRM system (Customer Relationship Management) is essential for managing and organizing follow-up in sales. An efficient CRM helps to track the history of interactions with customers, record important notes, schedule follow-ups, and ensure that no opportunities are missed. Additionally, a CRM can provide valuable analytics and information to help you better understand your customers and optimize your sales strategies.

Establish a follow-up process

Developing and implementing a well-defined follow-up process is essential to ensuring efficient and consistent follow-up. A follow-up process should include:

Defining follow-up goals

Identifying the best follow-up methods for each situation

Creating a follow-up schedule

Training your sales team in effective follow-up techniques

Monitoring and analyzing follow-up performance

Learning from your follow-ups

Analyzing the performance of your follow-ups and learning from them is crucial for continuous improvement of your sales strategies. Use customer feedback and data collected through your CRM to identify areas for improvement and adjust your approaches as necessary. Share best practices and lessons learned with your sales team to ensure everyone is aligned with the most effective follow-up techniques.

By understanding the importance of follow-up, choosing appropriate methods, creating relevant and personalized content, using an efficient CRM, establishing a follow-up process, and learning from your follow-ups, you can strengthen your customer relationships, increase satisfaction, generate additional sales, and improve customer retention.

Methods of follow-up

There are several ways to follow up with customers, and it is important to choose the most appropriate method for each situation. Some of the most common methods include email, phone, text messages, social media, and personal visits. Each method has its own advantages and disadvantages, and the choice of the correct method will depend on the customer's preferences, the nature of the relationship, and the message you want to convey.

Content of follow-up

The content of the follow-up should be relevant, personalized, and value-oriented. Avoid generic messages and focus on addressing the specific needs of the customer. Some tips for creating effective follow-up content include:

Thanking the customer for the purchase or interaction

Providing useful information or relevant updates to the customer

Addressing any concerns or questions the customer may have

Offering additional support or assistance, if necessary

Presenting opportunities for upselling or cross-selling in a helpful and appropriate manner

The importance of CRM (Customer Relationship Management)

The use of a CRM (Customer Relationship Management) system is essential for managing and organizing follow-up in sales. An efficient CRM helps to track the history of interactions with customers, record important notes, schedule follow-ups, and ensure that no opportunities are missed. In addition, a CRM can provide valuable analytics and insights to help you better understand your customers and optimize your sales strategies.

Establish a follow-up process

Developing and implementing a well-defined follow-up process is essential to ensure efficient and consistent follow-up. A follow-up process should include:

Defining follow-up goals

Identifying the best methods of follow-up for each situation

Creating a follow-up schedule

Training your sales team in effective follow-up techniques

Monitoring and analyzing follow-up performance

Learn from your follow-ups

Analyzing the performance of your follow-ups and learning from them is crucial for continuous improvement of your sales strategies. Use customer feedback and data collected through your CRM to identify areas for improvement and adjust your approaches as necessary.

Share best practices and lessons learned with your sales team to ensure everyone is aligned with the most effective follow-up techniques.

By understanding the importance of follow-up, choosing the appropriate methods, creating relevant and personalized content, utilizing an efficient CRM, establishing a follow-up process, and learning from your follow-ups, you can strengthen your relationship with your customers, increase satisfaction, generate additional sales, and improve customer retention.

Investing time and resources in developing effective follow-up skills and implementing strategies based on proven concepts and practices can result in a winning sales department and ensure the long-term success of your organization.

How to close more sales using the AIDA method

The AIDA method is a popular and effective sales framework that helps salespeople attract customer attention, spark interest, create desire, and motivate them to take action. The AIDA acronym stands for Attention, Interest, Desire, and Action.

Attention

The first step in the AIDA method is to capture the customer's attention. To do this, salespeople must be creative, stand out, and create an emotional connection with the customer. Some strategies to capture attention include:

> Using innovative and personalized approaches to start conversations;

> Sharing interesting and relevant stories about your product or service;

> Using clear and engaging language;

> Focusing on benefits and solutions, rather than just product features.

Interest

After capturing the customer's attention, the next step is to spark their interest. To do this, salespeople must present relevant and valuable information that connects to the customer's specific needs and desires. Some strategies to generate interest include:

Asking open-ended questions to better understand the customer's needs;

Providing detailed information about the benefits and advantages of your product or service;

Sharing case studies, testimonials, and success examples;

Establishing credibility and trust through social proof, such as reviews and recommendations.

Desire

The third step in the AIDA method is to create desire. To do this, salespeople must help customers visualize how the product or service can improve their lives or solve their problems.

Focusing on emotional and personal benefits associated with your product or service;

Using storytelling techniques to engage and emotionally connect with the customer;

Offering demonstrations, samples, or interactive experiences to allow customers to see the value of the product first-hand;

Using emotional triggers, such as urgency or exclusivity, to increase desire.

Action

The last step in the AIDA method is to motivate the customer to take action. To do this, salespeople must make the purchasing process easy, attractive, and risk-free. Some strategies to encourage action include:

Offering incentives, such as discounts or gifts, to motivate purchase;

Facilitating the purchasing process by removing barriers and simplifying steps;

Offering guarantees, return policies, and post-sales support to increase customer confidence;

Using effective closing techniques, such as assuming the sale or offering limited options.

Adapting the AIDA method to your sales process

To implement the AIDA method in your sales department, it is important to adapt it to the specific needs of your sales process and team. Consider the following steps to ensure a successful implementation:

Train your sales team on the AIDA method and explain the importance of each step;

Review and adjust your sales process to incorporate the four AIDA steps;

Monitor and evaluate your team's performance, identifying areas of improvement and success;

Encourage experimentation and innovation, allowing salespeople to test different approaches within the AIDA method;

Share best practices and lessons learned with the entire team to ensure continuous improvement.

Combining the AIDA method with other sales strategies

The AIDA method is an effective tool on its own, but can be even more powerful when combined with other validated sales strategies. Consider incorporating the following into your sales process, alongside the AIDA method:

Customer relationship focus: Build strong and lasting relationships with customers, ensuring their needs are met and they feel valued;

Consultative approach: Work together with the customer to identify and solve problems, presenting personalized and specific solutions;

Consistent follow-up: Ensure regular follow-up after the sale to maintain the customer relationship, solve problems, and identify additional sales opportunities.

The AIDA method is a proven and effective framework for closing more sales and improving the performance of your sales department.

Remember to combine the AIDA method with other validated sales strategies and share best practices with your team to ensure continuous growth and a winning sales department.

How to improve interpersonal communication in the sales team

A effective interpersonal communication is crucial for the success of any sales department. The ability to communicate clearly and build strong relationships, both internally and with customers, is an essential skill for salespeople.

Fostering a culture of open and honest communication

The foundation of effective interpersonal communication is a culture of openness and honesty. Encourage transparency and free expression of ideas and opinions within the sales team. This includes:

Establishing an open-door policy for discussions and feedback;

Encouraging collaboration and information exchange among team members;

Creating a safe environment where salespeople can share their concerns and challenges without fear of retaliation;

Promoting empathy and mutual understanding, encouraging the team to put themselves in each other's shoes.

Training in communication skills

Invest in training to help your sales team develop interpersonal communication skills. Offer training in areas such as:

Active listening: Learning to listen attentively and understand the needs and concerns of others;

Nonverbal communication: Understanding and using body language, tone of voice, and facial expressions to improve communication;

Emotional intelligence: Developing the ability to recognize and manage emotions, both in oneself and others;

Persuasion and influence techniques: Learning to ethically and effectively persuade and influence others.

Implementing effective communication tools

Leverage modern technologies to improve interpersonal communication within the sales team. Some tools that can help facilitate communication include:

Instant messaging platforms: Allow team members to exchange information and ideas quickly, even when working remotely;

Video conferencing software: Facilitate virtual meetings and group discussions, providing visual and auditory interaction;

Collaboration tools: Utilize apps and platforms that allow for real-time collaboration on documents and projects;

Project management systems: Implement solutions that help organize and monitor the progress of team tasks and projects.

Establishing clear communication channels

Ensure that all members of the sales team understand the available communication channels and how to use them properly. This may include:

Defining specific points of contact for different issues and concerns;

Creating clear guidelines on when and how to use different communication tools;

Establishing protocols for sharing sensitive or confidential information;

Encouraging regular communication between team members and sales department leaders.

Promoting interdepartmental communication

Improving interpersonal communication within the sales team also involves collaboration with other departments. Encourage open communication and teamwork between sales, marketing, customer support, and other relevant departments to ensure that everyone is aligned and working toward the same goals. Some ways to promote interdepartmental communication include:

Conducting regular interdepartmental meetings to discuss shared projects, goals, and challenges;

Establishing specific communication channels for interdepartmental collaboration;

Encouraging information exchange and resource sharing between teams;

Promoting team-building activities and events that include members from different departments.

Giving and receiving feedback constructively

Feedback is a crucial part of effective interpersonal communication. Encourage sales team members to give and receive feedback in a constructive and respectful manner. Some tips for effective feedback include:

Providing specific, fact-based feedback rather than personal opinions;

Focusing on behaviors and actions that can be changed rather than personal characteristics;

Using positive and encouraging language, even when addressing areas for improvement;

Being open to receiving feedback and willing to make changes based on colleagues' suggestions.

Improving interpersonal communication within the sales team is essential for the department's success and customer satisfaction.

Investing in training, promoting a culture of open and honest communication, and utilizing effective communication tools can help create a more cohesive and successful sales team. Establishing clear communication channels, encouraging interdepartmental collaboration, and addressing feedback constructively are important strategies for improving communication and driving overall sales department performance.

Consultative selling techniques

Consultative selling is a modern, customer-centric approach that focuses on identifying customer needs and offering personalized solutions. Instead of just trying to close deals, salespeople who adopt this approach act as trusted advisors, working together with the customer to solve problems and achieve results.

Adopt a consultant mindset

The foundation of consultative selling is the consultant mindset. Salespeople should focus on helping customers achieve their goals, rather than simply trying to sell a product or service. This includes:

> Learning about the industry and the customer's specific challenges;
>
> Asking questions to fully understand the customer's needs;
>
> Being honest and transparent in their recommendations and solutions;
>
> Providing ongoing value to the customer through support and follow-up.

Ask open and exploratory questions

Questions are a powerful tool in consultative selling. Asking open and exploratory questions helps to gather valuable information about the customer's needs and challenges. Some tips for asking effective questions include:

Ask open questions that encourage the customer to share information and ideas;

Avoid closed questions that can be answered with a simple "yes" or "no";

Focus on understanding the customer's goals, challenges, and concerns;

Use active listening techniques to ensure that you understand the customer's answers.

Demonstrate empathy and understanding

Empathy is critical in consultative selling. Demonstrating empathy and understanding for the customer's needs and concerns helps to build trust and establish a solid relationship. Some ways to show empathy include:

Validating the customer's emotions and concerns;

Putting yourself in the customer's shoes and considering their perspectives;

Sharing relevant experiences or stories to demonstrate understanding;

Expressing genuine concern and interest in the customer's well-being and success.

Offer personalized solutions

In consultative selling, it is essential to offer personalized and specific solutions to the customer's needs. This includes:

Analyzing the information gathered during conversations with the customer;

Developing solutions that address the customer's specific challenges and goals;

Presenting the solutions in a clear and understandable way, highlighting the benefits for the customer;

Adapting to changes in the customer's needs and adjusting solutions as necessary.

Establish long-term relationships

Consultative selling focuses on building long-term relationships with customers. This includes:

Staying in regular contact with customers to track their progress and provide support;

Providing additional resources and helpful information to help the customer achieve their goals;

Being available to answer questions and provide guidance as needed;

Anticipating the customer's future needs and presenting proactive solutions.

Focus on education, not selling

In consultative selling, it is important to focus on educating the customer rather than simply trying to close the sale. This can be done through:

Providing detailed and accurate information about the products or services offered;

Explaining how the proposed solutions align with the customer's needs and goals;

Using case studies, testimonials, and data to support your recommendations;

Encouraging the customer to ask questions and clarify their doubts.

Develop effective communication skills

Effective communication is critical in consultative selling. Salespeople should be able to communicate clearly and persuasively to present solutions and address customer concerns. Some tips for improving communication skills include:

Practicing active listening to fully understand the customer's needs;

Using clear and accessible language to explain solutions and benefits;

Refining presentation skills to deliver information in an engaging and persuasive way;

Adapting communication style to suit individual customer preferences and needs.

Consultative selling is an effective and customer-centric approach that can lead to significant results for your sales department. By adopting a consultant mindset, asking open and exploratory questions, demonstrating empathy and understanding, offering personalized solutions, and building long-term relationships, salespeople can become trusted advisors for their clients.

Focusing on education instead of sales and developing effective communication skills will help salespeople stand out and succeed in consultative selling. Implementing these techniques in your sales department can lead to greater customer satisfaction and long-term sales growth.

Sales strategies for the customer lifecycle

The customer lifecycle is an approach that considers the different stages that a customer goes through when interacting with a company, from the first contact to loyalty. Understanding and adapting sales strategies for each stage of the customer lifecycle is essential to ensure the success of the sales department and customer satisfaction.

Customer acquisition: attracting new customers

The first stage of the customer lifecycle is acquisition, where the goal is to attract new customers to the company. Some effective sales strategies for this stage include:

Develop targeted and segmented marketing campaigns to attract potential customers;

Use prospecting techniques, such as phone calls, emails, and networking events, to identify and contact potential customers;

Offer educational and informative content, such as webinars, e-books, and blog posts, to attract customers and show the value of your company;

Establish strategic partnerships with other companies to expand your reach in the market.

Lead conversion: turning prospects into paying customers

The second stage of the customer lifecycle is conversion, where the goal is to turn interested leads into paying customers. Effective sales techniques for this stage include:

Customer retention: keeping existing customers satisfied

The third stage of the customer lifecycle is retention, where the goal is to keep existing customers satisfied and continue to provide value. Effective sales strategies for this stage include:

Providing excellent customer service and post-sale support to ensure customers remain satisfied with your company;

Maintaining regular contact with customers to identify upsell and cross-sell opportunities;

Using customer surveys and feedback to identify areas for improvement and adapt your product or service offerings accordingly;

Implementing loyalty and rewards programs to encourage customers to continue doing business with your company.

Customer expansion: maximizing the value of existing customers

The fourth stage of the customer lifecycle is expansion, where the goal is to maximize the value of existing customers through upselling, cross-selling, and referrals. Effective sales strategies for this stage include:

Identifying upsell and cross-sell opportunities based on customer needs and purchase history;

Establishing regular communication with customers to discuss new products, services, or promotions that may be of interest;

Training your sales team to recognize and efficiently and ethically capitalize on expansion opportunities;

Encouraging referrals from satisfied customers by offering incentives and rewards for successful referrals.

Brand Champions: Turning Customers into Ambassadors

The fifth stage of the customer lifecycle is creating brand advocates, where the goal is to turn satisfied customers into ambassadors for your company. Effective sales strategies for this stage include:

Providing an exceptional customer experience in every interaction, ensuring that customers feel valued and appreciated;

Encouraging customers to share their positive experiences through testimonials, online reviews, and social media;

Monitoring and responding to customer feedback on social media and other communication channels to demonstrate that the company cares about customer satisfaction;

Developing marketing campaigns and events that engage customers and strengthen their connection to the brand.

Understanding and adapting sales strategies for each stage of the customer lifecycle is crucial for ensuring the success of the sales department and customer satisfaction. By implementing effective strategies to attract new customers, convert leads, retain and expand relationships with existing customers, and create brand advocates, your company will be well positioned to achieve sustainable growth and significant results.

Remember that the key to success at each stage of the customer lifecycle is to stay focused on the customer's needs and desires, providing personalized solutions and exceptional service.

How to measure and analyze the performance of the sales team.

Measuring and analyzing sales team performance is essential for the success of any sales department. The data generated by measuring sales team performance allows sales leaders to make informed decisions on how to improve the individual and collective performance of salespeople.

Sales Performance Metrics

Measuring sales team performance begins with identifying appropriate metrics. There are several metrics that sales leaders can use to evaluate salesperson performance. Some of the most common metrics include:

Revenue generated per salesperson;

Number of new customers acquired;

Sales conversion rate;

Average value of sales per transaction;

Customer retention rate.

These metrics provide an overview of sales team performance. However, it is important to remember that performance metrics should be specific to the business and objectives of the company. It is important to have a clear understanding of what is important to measure and why.

Data Analysis

Once performance metrics have been identified, it is important to analyze the data to better understand individual and collective salesperson performance. Modern data analysis tools can help sales leaders better understand salespeople behavior patterns and identify areas of opportunity for improving performance.

There are several data analysis tools that can be used to measure sales team performance. One of the most common tools is customer relationship management (CRM) software. The CRM allows sales leaders to capture important data about customer interactions and use that data to evaluate salesperson performance.

Another data analysis tool is sales conversation analysis. With this tool, sales leaders can analyze sales conversations between salespeople and customers to identify behavior patterns and areas of opportunity for improving performance.

Data analysis can also be used to identify sales trends and predict future demand. This information can be used to adjust sales strategies and ensure the sales team is prepared to meet demand.

Measuring and analyzing sales team performance is crucial for the success of any sales department. The correct performance metrics should be identified and analyzed with modern data analysis tools to gain valuable insights into sales team performance. These insights can be used to adjust sales strategies and ensure the team is working efficiently and effectively.

It is important to remember that measuring sales team performance should not be seen as a one-time or isolated process. Instead, it is an ongoing process that should be integrated into daily sales activities and reviewed regularly to ensure metrics are being properly evaluated and adjusted as needed.

Finally, to ensure that measuring and analyzing sales team performance is successful, it is important to involve the sales team in the process. They should be informed about the metrics being used and why they are important.

Additionally, it is important to provide regular feedback to salespeople on their individual and collective performance so they can adjust their daily activities and continuously improve.

Building a Sales Playbook

A sales playbook is a set of guidelines and processes that help the sales team to conduct the sales process consistently and effectively. Having a sales playbook is essential to ensure that the sales team is aligned with the company's sales objectives and that everyone is working with a common approach.

In this chapter, we will discuss how to build an effective sales playbook using modern concepts to ensure that the sales team is aligned and working consistently.

Defining the Sales Playbook Structure

Before starting to build a sales playbook, it is important to define the structure and components that will be present. An effective sales playbook should include the following sections:

Company and Product Overview: This section should provide an overview of the company and the products or services offered. It should include information about the company's history, mission, values, competitive differentiators, and details about the products or services that the company offers.

Buyer Personas: Buyer personas are fictional profiles that represent the ideal customer of the company. This section should describe the different buyer personas and how the company meets the needs of each one.

Sales Process: This section should describe the sales process of the company, from prospecting to closing. It should include information on how to identify qualified leads, how to conduct sales meetings, how to handle objections, and how to close a sale.

Common Objections: This section should describe the most common objections that salespeople face during the sales process and how to overcome them. Objections may include concerns about price, lack of need, competition, and other issues.

Sales Tools: This section should describe the sales tools that salespeople can use to help them close deals. The tools may include presentations, product demonstrations, case studies, and other marketing materials.

Sales Metrics: This section should describe the sales metrics that the company uses to measure the success of the sales team. Metrics may include the number of closed sales, sales conversion rate, revenue generated per salesperson, and other relevant metrics.

Developing the Sales Playbook

After defining the structure of the sales playbook, it's time to develop the content. This involves working with sales leaders and other team members to create the content that will be included in each section.

Here are some tips for developing the content of the sales playbook:

Work with the Sales Team: Involve the sales team in the sales playbook development process. They are the sales experts and can provide valuable information about the sales process and common objections faced during the sales process.

Personalize Buyer Personas: Buyer personas should be personalized to the company and its products or services. It's important to understand the needs and wants of customers to ensure that the sales playbook is effective.

Clearly Describe the Sales Process: The sales process should be described clearly and concisely. This will help the sales team to understand how to conduct a sale consistently and effectively.

Identify common objections: work with the sales team to identify the most common objections they face during the sales process. Describe how to overcome these objections and provide practical examples.

Include real-life examples: include real-life examples of successful sales to help the sales team understand how to apply the guidelines and processes described in the sales playbook.

Personalize sales tools: sales tools should be personalized for the company and its products or services. Include relevant and useful marketing materials to help the sales team close deals.

Define sales metrics: sales metrics should be clearly defined and concise. This will help the sales team understand how their performance is being measured and how they can improve.

Implementing the sales playbook

Once the sales playbook has been developed, it's time to implement it with the sales team. Here are some tips for ensuring effective implementation of the sales playbook:

Training: provide detailed training on the sales playbook to the sales team. They should understand how to use the sales playbook and how to apply the guidelines and processes described.

Monitoring and feedback: monitor the performance of the sales team and provide regular feedback on their performance. This will help identify areas for improvement and improve the performance of the team.

Updating the sales playbook: the sales playbook should be updated regularly to ensure that it remains relevant and effective. This may involve working with the sales team to identify areas for improvement and making adjustments to the sales playbook as necessary.

Building an effective sales playbook is essential for the success of the sales team and the company as a whole. A well-developed sales playbook should include an overview of the company and its products, buyer personas, sales process, common objections, sales tools, and sales metrics.

It's important to personalize the sales playbook for the company and its products or services, involve the sales team in the development process, and implement the sales playbook effectively. With an effective sales playbook, the sales team will be aligned with the company's sales goals and working consistently to close deals effectively.

How to use technology to increase sales team efficiency

Technology plays an increasingly important role in the success of the sales department. With the right tools, the sales team can work more efficiently, close more deals, and increase the company's revenue. In this chapter, we will discuss how to use technology to increase the efficiency of the sales team.

Sales Automation Tools

Sales automation tools can help the sales team work more efficiently and close more deals. These tools include:

CRM: Customer relationship management (CRM) software helps the sales team manage important customer information, including contact data, purchase history, and previous interactions. This allows salespeople to personalize their approach and provide better customer service.

Email automation: Email automation tools allow the sales team to send personalized mass emails to leads and customers. This helps to maintain communication with potential customers and reduces the time spent creating individual emails.

Workflow automation: Workflow automation tools help the sales team manage daily tasks, such as lead follow-up, scheduling meetings, and sending marketing materials. This allows salespeople to focus on the most important sales activities.

Sales Analytics Tools

Sales analytics tools can help the sales team better understand performance and identify opportunities for improvement. These tools include:

Sales conversation analysis: Sales conversation analysis tools allow sales leaders to analyze sales conversations between salespeople and customers to identify behavior patterns and areas of opportunity for improving performance.

Sales data analysis: Sales data analysis tools help the sales team better understand sales trends, identify areas of opportunity, and make informed decisions about sales strategy.

Individual performance analysis: Individual performance analysis tools allow sales leaders to analyze the individual performance of salespeople and identify areas for improvement.

Communication Tools

Communication tools help the sales team communicate with customers and the sales team efficiently. These tools include:

Video conferencing: Video conferencing tools allow the sales team to conduct virtual sales meetings with potential and existing customers. This helps to reduce travel costs and increase the efficiency of meetings.

Instant messaging: Instant messaging tools allow the sales team to communicate quickly and efficiently, which is particularly useful for remote teams or teams in different geographic locations.

Collaboration software: Collaboration tools help the sales team work together on projects and tasks, allowing salespeople to share ideas and work in real-time.

AI Tools: AI tools are increasingly present in the sales department, helping the team work more efficiently and effectively. These tools include:

Chatbots: Chatbots are computer programs that simulate human conversations. They can be used to answer common customer questions, schedule meetings, and even make sales.

Product recommendations: AI can be used to analyze a customer's purchase history and recommend additional products that may be of interest.

Sales forecasting: AI can be used to analyze sales data and market trends to predict future sales and identify sales opportunities.

The technological tools discussed in this chapter can help the sales team work more efficiently and effectively, increasing productivity and closing more deals. Sales automation, sales analytics, communication, and AI tools can help the sales team manage leads, personalize the sales approach, analyze sales data, and predict future sales opportunities.

As technology continues to evolve, it is important for companies to invest in the right tools to maximize the potential of the sales team.

Choosing the Best CRM for Your Company

Customer Relationship Management (CRM) system is an essential tool for any successful sales department. An efficient CRM allows your team to manage leads, track sales progress, and improve customer relationships. With so many CRM options available on the market, it can be challenging to determine which solution is best for your company.

Factors to consider when choosing a CRM

When choosing a CRM for your company, it's important to consider the following factors:

Functionality: The CRM should offer the features and functionality necessary to support your company's specific sales processes and goals.

Integration: The CRM should be able to seamlessly integrate with other tools and systems that your company already uses, such as marketing automation systems and customer service software.

Ease of use: The CRM should be intuitive and easy to use so that your sales team can start using it quickly and efficiently.

Customization: The CRM should be flexible enough to be customized according to your company's specific needs and preferences.

Scalability: The CRM should be able to grow with your company, allowing you to add features and functionality as needed.

Price: The CRM should fit within your company's budget and offer a good return on investment.

Top CRM solutions on the market currently

Here are some of the top CRM solutions available on the market currently:

Salesforce: Salesforce is one of the most popular and widely used CRMs, offering a wide range of features including lead management, sales automation, data analytics, and integration with a wide variety of apps and systems.

HubSpot CRM: HubSpot CRM is an easy-to-use and scalable CRM solution that offers lead management, sales automation, and data analytics features, along with seamless integration with other marketing and sales tools from HubSpot.

Zoho CRM: Zoho CRM is a comprehensive and customizable CRM solution that offers lead management, sales automation, data analytics, and integration with other Zoho tools and systems such as Zoho Desk and Zoho Mail.

Microsoft Dynamics 365 Sales: Microsoft Dynamics 365 Sales is an enterprise CRM solution that offers lead management, sales automation, data analytics, and integration with other Microsoft solutions such as Office 365 and Microsoft Teams.

Pipedrive: Pipedrive is a CRM designed specifically for sales teams, offering lead management, sales automation, and data analytics features, along with an intuitive and easy-to-use interface.

Testing and evaluating CRM solutions

Before making a final decision on the best CRM for your company, it's important to test and evaluate several solutions to ensure that you make the right choice.

Many CRM vendors offer free trials or demos, allowing you to try out their systems before committing. During the evaluation phase, be sure to involve your sales team in the process to get feedback on the ease of use and effectiveness of the tools in their daily activities.

How to use data to make smarter sales decisions

In today's world, data-driven decision-making is crucial to sales success. With the increasing amount of information available, companies have the opportunity to analyze and utilize this data to make more informed and effective sales decisions. Let's explore how to use data to improve sales decision-making, from identifying market opportunities to adjusting strategies and optimizing processes.

Identifying Market Opportunities

One of the most effective ways to use data to make smarter sales decisions is to analyze market trends and patterns to identify opportunities. This may include analyzing demographic, behavioral, and consumption data to identify market segments more likely to purchase your products or services. Additionally, analyzing historical sales data and seasonal data can help you predict future demands and allocate resources more efficiently.

Segmenting and Prioritizing Leads

Using data to segment and prioritize leads is another effective way to improve sales decision-making. By analyzing data about your leads' behavior and preferences, you can create more specific market segments and target your sales offers and messages accordingly. Analyzing engagement and interaction data can help you identify and prioritize leads more likely to convert, allowing your sales team to focus on the most promising leads.

Optimizing Sales Strategies

Sales data analysis can also help you optimize your sales strategies and improve your team's effectiveness. This may include analyzing sales performance data to identify strengths and weaknesses, as well as conducting A/B tests to determine the most effective sales tactics. Monitoring sales metrics and adjusting strategies based on results will help ensure that you are always making informed decisions and adapting to changes in market conditions.

Improving Sales Process Efficiency

Data can also be used to improve sales process efficiency by identifying bottlenecks and inefficiencies that may be hindering your team's success. This may include analyzing response time data, conversion rates, and average closing time to identify areas where improvements can be made. By addressing these issues and optimizing your sales process, you can increase your team's productivity and improve their results.

Monitoring and Adjusting Performance

Finally, it's important to use data to continuously monitor your sales team's performance and make adjustments as needed. This may include regularly analyzing key performance indicators (KPIs) to ensure that your team is meeting established goals and objectives. Using data to identify areas for improvement and providing targeted feedback and training to team members can help drive performance and motivation.

Using Data Analytics Tools and Technologies

To get the most out of data in your sales process, it's essential to use the right tools and technologies to collect, analyze, and visualize this information. Some CRM solutions, such as Salesforce, HubSpot, and Microsoft Dynamics 365, offer advanced data analysis features that make it easy to identify trends, patterns, and opportunities. Tools like Tableau, Power BI, and Google Data Studio can be useful for creating custom dashboards and interactive data visualizations that help communicate sales information more effectively.

Data-driven decision-making is essential for a winning sales department. By using data to identify market opportunities, segment and prioritize leads, optimize sales strategies, improve sales process efficiency, and monitor and adjust performance, you can make smarter sales decisions and drive your team's success.

By investing in data analytics tools and technologies, you'll be better equipped to harness the power of data and ensure that your sales department is always one step ahead of the competition.

The Role of Marketing in Generating Sales Leads

Lead generation is a critical component of a successful sales department. Without quality leads, the sales team will struggle to reach their goals and drive company growth. In this context, marketing plays a crucial role in lead generation and creating sales opportunities.

The importance of lead generation in marketing

Lead generation is one of the primary responsibilities of the marketing department. By creating campaigns and content that attract and engage the target audience, marketing creates opportunities for the sales team to connect with leads and convert them into customers. A successful lead generation process can help increase revenue, drive growth, and ensure long-term sustainability for the company.

Strategies and tactics for lead generation

There are several strategies and tactics that marketing professionals can use to generate leads and create sales opportunities. Some of these approaches include:

Content marketing: Creating and promoting relevant and valuable content (such as blog posts, e-books, whitepapers, and webinars) can attract and engage your target audience, establishing your company as a trusted source of information and generating leads in the process.

SEO (Search Engine Optimization): Optimizing your website and content for search engines can increase your company's online visibility, drive organic traffic, and generate high-quality leads.

Paid advertising: Using paid ads on search engines and social media platforms can help direct traffic to your landing pages, increase brand exposure, and generate leads quickly.

Social media: Promoting your brand and content on social media can help attract and engage your target audience, as well as generate leads through shares, comments, and interactions.

Email marketing: Email marketing campaigns can be used to nurture leads, share relevant content, and encourage conversion.

Nurturing leads and preparing them for the sales team

In addition to generating leads, marketing is also responsible for nurturing and preparing them for the sales team. This can include implementing lead nurturing programs that involve regularly sending relevant and personalized content, as well as using lead scoring and segmentation techniques to identify those who are ready to be approached by the sales team.

Aligning marketing and sales to maximize success

To ensure success in lead generation and sales conversion, it is crucial for the marketing and sales departments to be aligned and work together towards common goals. This can be achieved through clear and regular communication between the teams, establishing shared goals and performance metrics, and collaborating on lead generation strategies and tactics. Some steps to align marketing and sales include:

Generating leads is a critical component of a successful sales department. Without quality leads, the sales team will struggle to meet their goals and drive company growth. In this context, marketing plays a crucial role in lead generation and creating sales opportunities.

The importance of lead generation in marketing

Lead generation is one of the primary responsibilities of the marketing department. By creating campaigns and content that attract and engage the target audience, marketing creates opportunities for the sales team to connect with leads and convert them into customers. A successful lead generation process can help increase revenue, drive growth, and ensure long-term sustainability of the company.

Strategies and tactics for lead generation

There are several strategies and tactics that marketing professionals can use to generate leads and create sales opportunities. Some of these approaches include:

Content marketing: Creating and promoting relevant and valuable content (such as blog posts, e-books, whitepapers, and webinars) can attract and engage your target audience, establishing your company as a trusted source of information and generating leads in the process.

SEO (Search Engine Optimization): Optimizing your website and content for search engines can increase your company's online visibility, drive organic traffic, and generate high-quality leads.

Paid advertising: Using paid ads on search engines and social media platforms can help direct traffic to your landing pages, increase brand exposure, and generate leads quickly.

Social media: Promoting your brand and content on social media can help attract and engage your target audience, as well as generate leads through shares, comments, and interactions.

Email marketing: Email marketing campaigns can be used to nurture leads, share relevant content, and encourage conversion.

Nurturing leads and preparing them for the sales team

In addition to generating leads, marketing is also responsible for nurturing and preparing them for the sales team. This can include implementing lead nurturing programs that involve regular delivery of relevant and personalized content, as well as using lead segmentation and scoring techniques to identify those who are ready to be approached by the sales team.

Aligning marketing and sales to maximize success

To ensure success in lead generation and sales conversion, it is crucial for the marketing and sales departments to be aligned and work together towards common goals. This can be achieved through clear and regular communication between the teams, establishing shared goals and performance metrics, and collaborating on lead generation strategies and tactics. Some steps to align marketing and sales include:

Establishing a clear lead transfer process: Define a process for passing qualified leads from marketing to sales, including qualification criteria, lead scoring, and follow-up steps.

Sharing information and insights: Marketing and sales teams should regularly share information and insights about leads, customers, and market trends to ensure that both are working based on the most up-to-date and relevant information.

Defining shared goals and KPIs: Establish shared goals and key performance indicators (KPIs) that reflect the common objectives of marketing and sales, such as lead generation, sales conversion, and revenue.

Collaborating on campaigns and initiatives: Marketing and sales teams should work together to develop and execute campaigns and initiatives that generate leads and support the sales process, such as events, promotions, and content campaigns.

The role of marketing in lead generation is crucial to the success of a winning sales department. By developing and implementing effective lead generation strategies and tactics, nurturing and preparing leads for the sales team, and aligning marketing and sales efforts, companies can maximize the potential of their lead generation initiatives and drive growth and revenue.

By working together, marketing and sales departments can ensure that lead generation is a continuous and successful process, leading to impressive results for the entire company.

Developing a Marketing Strategy for Sales

An effective marketing strategy is crucial to the success of a sales department. The marketing strategy for sales is a plan aimed at attracting, engaging, and converting leads, supporting the sales team throughout the sales process. In this chapter, we will discuss the steps to develop a marketing strategy for sales, including setting goals, identifying the target audience, selecting tactics, and measuring performance.

Setting Marketing Goals for Sales

The first step in developing a marketing strategy for sales is to set clear and measurable goals. These goals should be specific, attainable, relevant, and time-based and may include goals related to lead generation, sales conversion, customer retention, or revenue growth.

Marketing goals for sales should align with the overall goals of the company and the sales department.

Identifying the Target Audience

The next step is to identify the target audience for your marketing strategy for sales. This involves analyzing demographic, psychographic, and behavioral information about your current and potential customers in order to create ideal buyer profiles.

These buyer profiles help the marketing team develop targeted messaging and content that resonates with the target audience and supports sales goals.

Creating a Marketing Plan for Sales

After selecting your marketing tactics and channels, it's time to create a detailed marketing plan for sales. This plan should include information about your goals, target audience, selected marketing tactics and channels, as well as a timeline and budget for implementing marketing activities.

It is also important to include details about coordination between the marketing and sales teams, ensuring an integrated and collaborative approach to achieving your goals.

Implementing the Marketing Strategy for Sales

With a detailed plan in hand, you can begin implementing your marketing strategy for sales. This involves creating and promoting content, optimizing your website and social media, executing email marketing and paid advertising campaigns, and monitoring results.

During implementation, it is essential that the marketing and sales teams work together to ensure efficient transfer of qualified leads and to adjust marketing activities as necessary.

Measuring Performance of the Marketing Strategy for Sales

To ensure the success of your marketing strategy for sales, it is crucial to measure its performance and adjust tactics and approaches as necessary. This involves tracking key performance metrics (KPIs) such as lead generation, conversion rate, cost per lead, sales cycle, and marketing return on investment (ROI).

Analyzing these metrics can help identify areas of success and opportunities for improvement, allowing you to optimize your marketing strategy for sales and maximize impact on your sales goals.

Developing a marketing strategy for sales involves setting clear goals, identifying the target audience, selecting effective marketing tactics and channels, creating a detailed plan, and implementing and measuring the performance of the strategy.

By following these steps and working closely with the sales team, you can create a marketing strategy for sales that supports the success of your sales department and contributes to the growth and profitability of your company.

How to create relevant content for your audience

Content marketing is an essential part of any successful marketing and sales strategy. Creating relevant and engaging content helps attract, nurture, and convert leads, as well as establish your company as an authority in your industry.

Researching industry topics and trends

To create relevant content, it's essential to start with solid research. This involves investigating topics and trends in your industry, as well as the interests and needs of your audience. Some ways to research topics and trends include:

Monitoring online forums and discussion groups related to your industry;

Keeping up with industry news and developments;

Reading influential blogs and publications in your field;

Conducting keyword research to identify popular and relevant terms.

This research will help identify areas of interest for your audience and provide insights into the topics that are most relevant and appealing.

Identifying the needs and interests of your audience

When creating relevant content, it's important to understand the specific needs and interests of your audience. This can be done through market research, analysis of demographic and behavioral data, and direct customer feedback.

By identifying the needs and interests of your audience, you can create content that addresses these areas and provides real value to readers.

Producing engaging and informative content

With a clear understanding of industry topics and trends and the needs of your audience, you can begin producing engaging and informative content. Some tips for creating relevant content include:

Focusing on quality over quantity: Invest time and resources in creating high-quality content that provides valuable information and insights to readers.

Being original and authentic: Avoid overusing jargon and cliches and instead adopt an authentic and original voice that reflects the personality and values of your brand.

Using a variety of content formats: Experiment with different content formats, such as blogs, videos, webinars, e-books, and info graphics, to keep your audience engaged and interested.

Including stories and examples: Stories are a powerful way to engage your audience and illustrate important points. Include real-life examples and stories to make your content more relevant and captivating.

Optimizing your content for SEO

Relevant content is not just about what you write but also how you present it. Optimizing your content for SEO (Search Engine Optimization) is an important part of creating relevant content, ensuring that your audience can easily find it on search engines. Some tips for optimizing your content for SEO include:

Researching and using relevant keywords: Identify the most relevant keywords for your topic and include them naturally and strategically throughout your content.

Creating compelling titles and headlines: Use titles and headlines that are interesting and informative and that include your keywords.

Optimizing meta tags and descriptions: Write compelling and relevant meta tags and descriptions that include your keywords and encourage users to click on your content.

Including internal and external links: Add links to other pages on your site and relevant external sources to improve the user experience and increase the authority of your content.

Promoting and sharing your content

After creating relevant and SEO-optimized content, it's important to promote and share it with your audience. Some strategies for promoting and sharing your content include:

Using social media: Share your content on relevant social media platforms and encourage your audience to share and interact with the content.

Sending email newsletters: Include your content in email newsletters to inform your audience about new features and keep them engaged.

Collaborating with influencers and industry partners: Work with influencers and industry partners to expand the reach of your content and attract new audiences.

Attending events and conferences: Present your content at industry events and conferences to increase visibility and establish your authority on the subject.

Creating relevant content for your audience is essential to the success of your marketing and sales strategies. By researching industry topics and trends, identifying audience needs, producing engaging and informative content, optimizing for SEO, and promoting and sharing your content, you can attract and nurture leads and establish your company as an authority in your field. This, in turn, will result in a more effective and successful sales department.

Using social media to generate sales leads

Social media has become an increasingly important tool for businesses to generate leads and develop relationships with potential customers. Here, we will explore how to use social media to generate sales leads, addressing specific strategies, the importance of audience segmentation, and how to measure the success of your social media campaigns.

Choosing the right platforms

The first step in using social media to generate sales leads is to choose the most suitable platforms for your company and target audience. Some of the main platforms include Facebook, Instagram, LinkedIn, Twitter, and YouTube. Each platform has its own set of features and target audience, so it's important to select those that best align with your sales goals and the profile of your audience.

Audience segmentation

Segmenting your audience is key to generating quality sales leads on social media. By targeting your content and campaigns to a specific audience, you will increase the relevance and effectiveness of your marketing efforts. To segment your audience effectively, consider the following factors:

Demographics: age, gender, location, income, and education.

Behavior: interests, hobbies, lifestyle, and buying behavior.

Needs and challenges: identify the problems and challenges your audience faces and how your company can help solve them.

Specific strategies for generating sales leads on social media

There are several strategies you can use to generate sales leads on social media. Some of these strategies include:

Sharing valuable and informative content: create and share relevant content that addresses the needs and interests of your target audience. This will help establish your company as an authority in your industry and attract leads interested in your products or services.

Engaging with your audience: respond to comments, questions, and messages from your audience on social media. This demonstrates that your company cares about its customers and is available to help them.

Promoting exclusive offers and promotions: use social media to offer discounts, promotions, and exclusive offers to your followers. This will encourage action and help generate sales leads.

Using paid advertising: take advantage of the advanced targeting available on social media platforms to promote your products and services directly to your target audience through paid ads.

Integrating social media and other marketing strategies

To achieve better results in generating sales leads, it's important to integrate your social media strategies with other marketing actions, such as content marketing, email marketing, and SEO. This will provide a more holistic approach and increase the likelihood of converting leads into customers. Some ways to integrate social media into your other marketing strategies include:

Sharing your blog content: when you publish a new blog post, share it on social media to increase its visibility and attract more leads.

Encouraging newsletter subscriptions: use your social media platforms to promote your email newsletter and encourage followers to subscribe.

Collaborating with influencers: work with influencers in your industry to create and share content on their respective social media platforms. This will expand the reach of your content and help attract new leads.

Harnessing the power of groups and communities: participate in groups and communities on social media that are relevant to your industry and target audience. Share your knowledge and establish relationships with other members to generate leads.

Measuring the success of your social media campaigns

To ensure that your social media strategies are effective in generating sales leads, it's important to measure and analyze their performance. Some important metrics to monitor include:

Engagement: audience engagement with your content on social media, such as likes, comments, and shares, is a good indicator of interest and can lead to sales leads.

Conversions: track how many social media leads convert into customers. This will help you determine the effectiveness of your campaigns and adjust your strategies as needed.

Cost per lead: calculate the acquisition cost of each lead generated through your social media campaigns. This will help you determine if your strategies are profitable and identify areas for improvement.

Return on Investment (ROI): Monitor your social media campaigns' ROI to ensure that you are getting a positive return on your marketing investment.

Social media is a powerful tool for generating sales leads and establishing relationships with potential customers. By choosing the appropriate platforms, segmenting your audience, implementing specific lead generation strategies, integrating your social media actions with other marketing strategies, and measuring your campaigns' success, you will be on the right track to building a winning sales department.

Remember to always test and adjust your approaches to continue improving your results and achieving success in your sales.

Strategies to optimize your website for sales

Your website is an essential tool for generating leads, building relationships with potential customers, and closing sales. Therefore, it is crucial that you optimize your site to ensure it is effective in converting visitors into customers.

Responsive design

A responsive design is critical to ensure your site is accessible and works well on all devices, including desktops, tablets, and smartphones. A responsive site adjusts its layout and content automatically based on the device screen size, providing a pleasant and consistent user experience. This is especially important as more consumers use mobile devices to research products and services.

Intuitive navigation

Your site's navigation should be clear and easy to use, allowing visitors to quickly find the information they are looking for. Some tips to improve your site's navigation include:

Organize your content into logical and hierarchical categories;

Include a visible main menu on all pages;

Offer a search function to help visitors find specific information;

Use clear headings and subheadings to facilitate reading and comprehension.

Clear calls-to-action (CTAs)

Effective CTAs are crucial for converting visitors into leads and customers. Some tips for creating clear and effective CTAs include:

Use contrasting colors to make the CTAs stand out in your site's design

Choose action words that encourage visitors to act (e.g., "Download now," "Contact us," or "Buy now")

Place CTAs in strategic locations throughout your site, such as in the header, at the end of blog posts, and on product pages.

Relevant and valuable content

Your site's content should be relevant and valuable to your target audience, addressing their needs, challenges, and interests. Quality content not only attracts visitors to your site but also helps them make informed decisions about your products or services. Additionally, good content can improve your search engine presence and increase your online visibility. Some tips for creating relevant content include:

Regularly publish blog posts that address topics of interest to your audience

Create detailed product pages that highlight your product's features, benefits, and specifications

Offer useful resources, such as e-books, whitepapers, and videos, that add value and educate your audience.

Testimonials and case studies: Include testimonials from satisfied customers and successful case studies to increase your brand's credibility and demonstrate the value of your products or services.

Search engine optimization (SEO)

Search engine optimization (SEO) is essential to ensure your site is easily found by potential customers. Some SEO best practices include:

Conducting keyword research to identify the most relevant and popular terms for your audience;

Incorporating keywords naturally and strategically throughout your content;

Optimizing on-page elements, such as titles, meta descriptions, and URLs;

Obtaining high-quality backlinks from reputable, industry-related sites;

Monitoring and analyzing your site traffic and adjusting your SEO strategies as needed.

Implementation of analytics and performance tracking.

Tracking and analyzing your site's performance is critical to identifying areas for improvement and ensuring your optimization strategies are effective. Use analytical tools, such as Google Analytics, to measure important metrics such as site traffic, average time on page, bounce rate, and conversions.

This information can help you better understand visitor behavior and adjust your sales optimization strategies as needed.

Optimizing your site for sales is an ongoing process that requires attention to detail and the ability to adapt to changes in audience preferences and market trends. By implementing the strategies mentioned in this chapter, you'll be on the right track to transform your site into a powerful sales tool and ensure the success of your sales department.

Remember to continually monitor your site's performance and adjust your strategies as needed to stay current and relevant to your target audience.

How to use email marketing to generate sales

Email marketing is a powerful and cost-effective tool that can help generate sales and increase customer retention. It allows you to connect directly with your customer base, build relationships, and effectively promote your products and services.

Build a quality email list

The first step to email marketing success is building a quality email list, made up of potential and existing customers who have shown interest in your brand and products. Some ways to build an email list include:

Adding a sign-up form on your website and blog

Offering an incentive to sign up, such as a discount or free e-book

Collecting email addresses at events and trade shows

Integrating email sign-up into your sales and customer service processes.

Remember that quality is more important than quantity when building your email list. It's better to have a smaller list of engaged subscribers than a larger list of people who aren't interested in your content.

Create segmented campaigns

To increase the effectiveness of your email marketing campaigns, it's important to segment your email list based on specific criteria, such as location, purchase history, or interests. This allows you to personalize your content and offers to better meet the needs of each segment. Segmented campaigns often have higher open and conversion rates because the content is more relevant and appealing to the recipient.

Develop relevant and valuable content

Your email marketing content should be relevant and valuable to your subscribers. This can include information about new products, special offers, helpful tips, and customer success stories. Quality content will help build trust and relationships with your customer base, increasing the likelihood that they will become loyal customers and make purchases.

Use a compelling subject line

The subject line is one of the most important elements of an email marketing message because it's the first thing recipients see. A compelling and relevant subject line increases the likelihood that your emails will be opened and read. Some tips for creating effective subject lines include:

Keep subject lines short and to the point

Use words and phrases that spark interest and curiosity

Personalize the subject line by including the recipient's name when appropriate

Test and optimize your campaigns.

To ensure the success of your email marketing campaigns, it's important to continuously test and optimize your emails and strategies. This can include A/B testing different subject lines, email designs, content, and offers. Monitor and analyze the results of your campaigns, such as open rates, clicks, and conversions, to identify areas for improvement and adjust your strategies as necessary.

Establish an appropriate sending frequency

Finding the ideal email sending frequency is crucial for maintaining subscriber engagement and avoiding unsubscribes. Sending emails too frequently can lead to subscriber burnout, while sending emails too infrequently can cause your brand to be forgotten. Consider starting with a monthly or biweekly frequency and adjust as necessary based on subscriber feedback and campaign performance.

Automate follow-up emails

Email marketing automation is an efficient way to maintain customer engagement and increase sales without overwhelming your sales team. Use specific triggers, such as website actions or important dates, to send automated follow-up emails. For example, you can send abandoned cart emails to remind customers to complete their purchases or birthday emails with special offers to celebrate the occasion.

Integrate email marketing with other sales strategies

Email marketing should be an integral part of your overall sales strategy, working together with other tactics such as social media, SEO, and content marketing. This will help ensure a holistic and cohesive approach to reaching and converting potential customers.

Email marketing is a proven sales strategy that can generate significant results when implemented correctly. By following the best practices and strategies discussed in this chapter, you'll be on your way to creating successful email marketing campaigns and driving sales in your sales department.

Continuously test and adjust your campaigns to ensure that you're meeting the needs and preferences of your evolving customer base.

Developing an upsell and cross-sell strategy

In a winning sales department, it is essential to maximize the revenue generated from each customer. Two effective strategies to achieve this goal are upselling and cross-selling. Upselling involves selling a higher-value product or service to the customer, while cross-selling involves selling complementary products or services.

The importance of upselling and cross-selling:

Maximizing customer value: Upselling and cross-selling allow you to extract more value from each customer, increasing your revenue and improving the return on investment in customer acquisition.

Improving customer retention: By offering additional products and services that meet the needs and desires of your customers, you can improve their satisfaction and loyalty, leading to greater customer retention.

Optimizing resource usage: As you already have a relationship with your existing customers, the cost and effort to sell to them through upselling and cross-selling are generally lower than acquiring new customers.

Identifying upsell and cross-sell opportunities:

Analyze your portfolio of products and services: Identify which products or services can be bundled or offered as a higher-value proposition. Consider how different products or services in your portfolio can complement or enhance each other.

Know your customers: Understand the needs, desires, and behavior patterns of your customers. This will allow you to identify upsell and cross-sell opportunities that are relevant and valuable to them.

Monitor customer behavior: Use purchase data and customer interactions to identify patterns and opportunities for upselling and cross-selling. For example, if a customer has purchased a specific product, what other complementary products or services may they be interested in?

Developing an upsell and cross-sell strategy:

Set clear goals: Establish specific, measurable, achievable, relevant, and time-bound (SMART) goals for your upselling and cross-selling initiatives. These goals should be aligned with your overall sales and business objectives.

Create compelling offers: Develop upsell and cross-sell offers that are attractive and valuable to your customers. Consider offering discounts, packages, or exclusive benefits to encourage customers to take advantage of these offers.

Train your sales team: Ensure that your sales team understands the importance of upselling and cross-selling and is well-trained to identify and capitalize on these opportunities. Provide them with the information and tools they need to successfully present these offers to customers.

Communicate effectively: Communicate your upsell and cross-sell offers to customers in a clear and persuasive manner. Use multiple communication channels, such as email, phone, and social media, to reach your customers and ensure they are aware of the offers available.

Monitor and adjust your strategy: Monitor the performance of your upselling and cross-selling initiatives and adjust your strategy as needed. Analyze conversion rates, average order value, and customer satisfaction to identify areas for improvement and optimize your approach.

Examples of successful upsell and cross-sell:

Software companies: Software companies often offer different levels of their products or services, with varying features and prices. They can encourage upselling by highlighting the benefits of a more advanced plan, such as more storage, additional features, or priority support.

E-commerce: Online stores can use cross-selling by suggesting related products based on the customer's purchase history or views. For example, if a customer is buying a laptop, the store can suggest a mouse, backpack, or antivirus software as complementary products.

Telecom companies: Telecom providers can offer upsells through larger data plans or additional services, such as device insurance or family plans. They can also employ cross-selling by offering accessories, such as headphones or protective cases, during the purchase of a smartphone.

Developing an effective upsell and cross-sell strategy is a powerful way to maximize customer value and drive growth for your organization.

By identifying opportunities, creating compelling offers, and communicating them effectively, your sales team can leverage the potential of upselling and cross selling to increase revenue and strengthen customer relationships.

How to create and maintain long-lasting relationships with customers

A winning sales department not only attracts new customers but also works hard to maintain long-lasting relationships with existing customers. Establishing and maintaining these strong relationships is essential to the long-term success of your business.

After all, satisfied customers are more likely to do repeat business and refer your company to others. Here, we will explore how to create and maintain long-lasting customer relationships using modern techniques and easily understandable language.

First and foremost, it is important to understand that the foundation of any lasting relationship is trust. When customers trust your company, they feel more comfortable continuing to do business with you. To build that trust, follow these steps:

Be transparent: Always be honest and open with your customers about your products, services, and prices. When customers feel they are receiving clear and accurate information, they trust your company more.

Keep your promises: Always deliver what you promised, be it a delivery time, a level of quality, or a specific outcome. When customers perceive you as reliable, they are more likely to maintain a long-term relationship with your company.

Be responsive and accessible: Always be available to answer your customers' questions and concerns. When customers feel they can contact your company and get quick answers, they feel more secure and confident in their relationship with you.

Personalize the customer experience: Demonstrate that you truly care about your customers by getting to know them and personalizing your interactions with them. This can include using the customer's name, remembering their preferences, or even sending personalized messages on special occasions.

Solicit feedback and listen to your customers: Show customers that you value their opinion and are willing to learn from them. Ask for feedback regularly and use that information to improve your products, services, and processes.

Resolve problems efficiently: When problems or conflicts arise, address them promptly and professionally. Resolving problems quickly and satisfactorily is essential to maintaining customer trust.

Establish emotional connections: People tend to be loyal to companies that provide them with positive emotional experiences. To create those connections, make customers feel valued, appreciated, and understood.

To maintain long-lasting relationships with customers, it is crucial to invest in quality service and support. This means ensuring your team is well-trained and equipped to provide the best possible experience to customers.

Additionally, remember to continue improving your products and services, adapting to changes in customer needs and expectations. This way, you demonstrate your commitment to providing innovative and valuable solutions to your customers.

Another important aspect of maintaining long-lasting relationships is continuous and effective communication. Keep in regular contact with your customers through emails, newsletters, social media, and other communication channels. By sharing relevant and useful information, you help keep your company at the forefront of customers' minds.

Recognize and reward customer loyalty. This can include offering exclusive discounts, loyalty programs, or special promotions for loyal customers. These rewards not only encourage customers to continue doing business with your company, but also make them feel valued and appreciated.

Don't forget to celebrate customers' achievements and milestones. Recognize their accomplishments and show that you are genuinely interested in their success. This can involve sending congratulations messages for a new job, birthdays, or other important achievements in customers' lives.

Last but not least, be flexible and willing to adapt to changes in customer needs and preferences. The business world is constantly evolving, and to maintain long-lasting relationships, it is essential to keep up with these changes and adjust your approach accordingly.

Creating and maintaining long-lasting customer relationships requires a customer-centric approach, based on trust, effective communication, and continuous support. By adopting these practices and striving to provide the best possible experience to customers, you establish strong and lasting relationships that benefit your business in the long run.

How to deal with unhappy customers

Dealing with dissatisfied customers is an inevitable challenge in the world of sales. However, it is crucial to approach these situations in an effective and professional manner, turning a negative moment into a learning and growth opportunity. In this chapter, we will discuss how to handle dissatisfied customers in a productive and constructive way, using easy-to-understand language.

The first step in dealing with a dissatisfied customer is to listen carefully to their concerns. Allow the customer to express their frustrations without interrupting or becoming defensive. Often, customers just want to be heard and feel that their concerns are being taken seriously. Show empathy and understanding when listening, demonstrating that you care about the customer's problem and are committed to finding a solution.

After fully understanding the issue, take responsibility for the problem, even if you are not directly responsible. This shows the customer that your company is committed to resolving the problem and that you are not trying to pass the blame. Apologize sincerely and then focus on finding a solution that can remedy the situation.

While working to resolve the problem, it is important to act quickly and efficiently. If the customer has been waiting a long time for a resolution, they may become even more dissatisfied and lose confidence in your company. Inform the customer about the next steps and provide a realistic timeline for the problem to be resolved.

As you work on the solution, keep the customer informed about the progress. Regular and transparent communication is essential to maintaining the customer's trust and showing that you are committed to resolving the situation. If there are delays or changes to the plan, inform the customer as soon as possible.

Once the problem has been resolved, follow up with the customer to ensure that they are satisfied with the solution. This demonstrates your commitment to ensuring customer satisfaction and can help restore trust in your company. Additionally, ask for feedback on how the situation was handled and use this information to improve your processes and prevent future problems.

Finally, it is crucial to learn from the experiences of dissatisfied customers. Analyze what went wrong and identify any areas that can be improved. Use these insights to adjust your practices and team training, ensuring that your company is always evolving and improving.

Dealing with dissatisfied customers can be a challenging experience, but by facing the situation in a professional and empathetic manner, it is possible to turn a negative moment into a learning and growth opportunity. Adopting a customer-centered approach and working to resolve problems efficiently and effectively will help ensure customer satisfaction and long-term loyalty.

Throughout your sales career, you are likely to encounter a variety of situations involving dissatisfied customers. Therefore, it is essential to develop solid problem-solving skills and improve your ability to deal with stress and pressure in such situations.

An important skill to develop is the ability to remain calm and composed, even when confronted with an angry or frustrated customer. Remember that, in most cases, the customer's anger is not directed at you personally, but rather at the situation. Take deep breaths, maintain a calm and professional tone of voice, and remember that your main goal is to solve the problem and restore customer satisfaction.

Another effective strategy is to establish and maintain clear boundaries. While it is important to address customer concerns and work to find a solution, it is also crucial to ensure that you are not being treated disrespectfully or abusively. If a customer becomes aggressive or disrespectful, stay calm and inform them that you are willing to help, but you expect to be treated with respect. Setting firm and fair boundaries can help keep the situation under control and ensure that you are treated with dignity and professionalism.

It is also useful to have an internal support system within your organization. This may include colleagues, supervisors, or managers who can provide guidance, support, and additional resources to help resolve complex or challenging problems. Do not hesitate to seek the support and help of your team, as this can be essential in dealing with unsatisfied customers effectively.

Finally, remember that each interaction with an unsatisfied customer is an opportunity to learn and improve your sales and customer service skills. Analyze each situation carefully and identify any lessons that can be learned. By doing so, you will be constantly improving your skills and becoming a more effective and successful sales professional.

By adopting an empathetic and customer-centered approach and using effective problem-solving skills, you can transform challenging interactions with unsatisfied customers into valuable learning experiences. These skills will not only help ensure customer satisfaction and loyalty, but also contribute to your growth and success as a sales professional.

How to obtain customer feedback and use it to improve sales

Obtaining feedback from customers is a vital part of the sales process, as it allows you to identify areas for improvement and adjust your approach to better meet the customer's needs and expectations.

Firstly, it is important to create an environment in which customers feel comfortable sharing their opinions and feedback. This can be achieved by demonstrating empathy, asking open-ended questions, and listening attentively to customer responses. Make it clear that you value their opinion and are willing to act on their suggestions and concerns.

Additionally, it is essential to be proactive in seeking feedback. Don't wait for customers to approach you with their opinions; instead, take the initiative to contact them and ask specific questions about their experience. You can do this through satisfaction surveys, phone calls, or emails.

Make sure to include questions that address different aspects of the sales process, such as customer service, product quality, and effectiveness of sales communications.

When receiving feedback, it is crucial to approach it with an open and receptive mindset. Avoid being defensive or justifying your actions, as this can discourage the customer from sharing their opinions in the future. Instead, thank the customer for their feedback and assure them that you will do your best to address their concerns.

After collecting feedback, it is important to analyze it and identify patterns and trends. This will allow you to determine which areas require improvement and develop specific strategies to address these issues. For example, if multiple customers comment that the checkout process on your website is confusing, this may indicate the need to simplify and improve the user experience.

Finally, it is crucial to act on the feedback received. This may include adjusting your sales approach, improving the quality of your products or services, or investing in additional training for your team.

By implementing changes based on customer feedback, you demonstrate that you are committed to providing an exceptional experience and are willing to adapt to the needs and expectations of your customers.

Customer feedback is a valuable tool that can help you identify areas for improvement and adjust your sales approach to meet your customers' needs.

By creating a receptive environment, proactively seeking feedback, and acting on the information collected, you will be better positioned to optimize your sales process and achieve increasingly better results.

In addition to the strategies mentioned above, there are other ways to collect and utilize customer feedback to improve your sales and customer experience. Let's explore some of these additional approaches.

Monitor social media: Social media is an excellent channel for keeping track of conversations about your brand and products. Pay attention to customer discussions and comments to identify areas for improvement and opportunities to enhance your sales strategy.

Conduct personal interviews: Personal interviews with customers can provide detailed information about their experiences and perceptions. Dedicate time to talk to customers, whether by phone or in person, and ask about their experiences and any suggestions for improvements they may have.

Organize focus groups: Focus groups are meetings with a select number of customers to discuss specific aspects of your products or services. These sessions can help you obtain direct and detailed feedback, allowing you to make more informed adjustments to your sales strategy.

Analyze performance metrics: Keep a close eye on performance metrics, such as conversion rates, average sales time, and customer satisfaction. This will help identify areas that need improvement and allow you to adjust your sales approach accordingly.

Implement a continuous feedback system: Establish a process for collecting and analyzing real-time customer feedback. This will allow you to quickly identify problem areas and make adjustments to your sales strategy as needed.

Share feedback with your team: Make sure to share customer feedback with your sales team and other relevant areas of the company. This will ensure that everyone is aware of customer expectations and works together to address areas of concern.

Monitor progress: After implementing changes based on customer feedback, closely monitor the results to ensure that the improvements are effective. If necessary, make additional adjustments and continue to refine your sales strategy.

By incorporating these additional approaches into your customer feedback collection and utilization strategy, you will be even better prepared to make informed decisions that drive sales success. Remember that customer feedback is a valuable resource and, when used properly, can provide invaluable insights for improving your sales and customer satisfaction.

The role of customer service in sales success

Excellent customer service not only ensures that customers are satisfied with your products and services, but also builds lasting relationships, generates trust and loyalty, and can lead to repeat sales and referrals.

The Importance of Customer Service in Sales

Customer satisfaction: A satisfied customer is more likely to continue doing business with your company and recommend your products and services to others. Ensuring that your customers are satisfied with your customer service can be a determining factor for the success of sales.

Brand loyalty: Good customer service contributes to building brand loyalty. When customers feel valued and well-served, they tend to continue buying from a company and, in turn, increase sales success.

Word-of-mouth advertising: Satisfied and loyal customers are more likely to share their positive experiences with friends, family, and colleagues, generating word-of-mouth advertising. This can lead to new customers and additional sales.

Reduced complaints and returns: Efficient customer service can help reduce complaints and returns from unhappy customers. By resolving problems quickly and effectively, companies can maintain customer satisfaction and minimize the negative impact on sales.

Additional sales and upselling: Good customer service can help identify opportunities for additional sales and upselling, further increasing sales. When customers are satisfied with the service they receive, they are more open to exploring other offerings and products from the company.

Strategies to Improve Customer Service and Boost Sales

Train your team: The customer service team should be trained to listen carefully to customers, understand their concerns, and offer effective solutions. Invest in continuous training to ensure that your team is always up to date with the best customer service practices.

Communicate clearly and effectively: Clear and effective communication is essential for quality customer service. Make sure your customer service team understands the products and services your company offers and can communicate this information easily and understandably to customers.

Be available to your customers: Offer multiple communication channels for your customers, such as phone, email, live chat, and social media. This allows customers to contact your company conveniently and helps ensure that their needs are met promptly.

Resolve problems quickly: Quick problem resolution is essential for good customer service. Establish efficient and effective processes for resolving issues and responding to customer concerns as quickly as possible.

Personalize service: Personalized service helps create stronger connections with customers and increases customer satisfaction. Encourage your customer service team to use the customer's name during interactions and to adapt their approaches to meet the specific needs of each customer.

Monitor and measure customer service performance: Implement key performance indicators (KPIs) and metrics to measure the effectiveness of customer service and identify areas for improvement. Regularly analyze this data and adjust your customer service strategies as needed to ensure sales success.

Ask for customer feedback: Soliciting customer feedback can help identify areas for improvement in customer service and, in turn, drive sales. Encourage customers to share their experiences and use this information to improve your customer service and sales strategies.

Creating a customer-centric culture is key to ensuring that customer service is a priority in your company. This involves encouraging empathy, accountability, and open communication among employees and ensuring that everyone understands the importance of customer service in the success of sales.

Customer service plays a critical role in sales success and, when implemented correctly, can lead to a significant increase in revenue and customer loyalty. Invest time and resources in training your customer service team, implementing effective customer service strategies, and creating a customer-centric culture to ensure that your company is successful in the competitive world of sales.

How to develop a sales culture in the company

Sales culture is a set of shared values, beliefs, behaviors, and practices that shape how a company approaches sales and customer interactions. A strong and positive sales culture can be a competitive differentiator and significantly contribute to a company's success.

Define clear values and goals

The first step in developing a sales culture is to establish clear values and goals for the company and its sales team. These values and goals should be customer-centric and reflect the company's mission and vision. Additionally, it is essential to communicate these values and goals to all employees and ensure they are aligned with the overall company strategy.

Establish efficient processes and systems

A successful sales culture requires efficient processes and systems that enable the sales team to achieve their goals and maximize their performance. This may include implementing an effective CRM, establishing a standardized sales process, and creating a system of metrics and key performance indicators (KPIs) to evaluate progress.

Invest in sales team development and training

The success of a sales culture depends largely on the skills and competencies of the sales team. Therefore, it is essential to invest in ongoing development and training for employees, ensuring they have the necessary skills to perform their tasks efficiently and effectively. Additionally, regular training can help keep employees motivated and engaged.

Foster collaboration and communication between teams

A strong sales culture is based on effective collaboration and communication between teams and departments within the company. This may include creating open and transparent communication between the sales and marketing teams, promoting team-building activities, and creating an inclusive and welcoming work environment.

Celebrate successes and learn from failures

To develop a successful sales culture, it is important to recognize and celebrate the sales team's and individual employees' achievements. This may include creating recognition and reward programs, as well as promoting events and celebrations to commemorate success. Additionally, it is important to learn from failures and identify areas for improvement to ensure the company and sales team's continuous growth.

Promote accountability and self-discipline

An effective sales culture requires accountability and self-discipline from all employees. It is essential that each team member understands their role and responsibilities and is committed to achieving their goals and objectives. To promote accountability and self-discipline, company leaders should set clear expectations, provide regular and constructive feedback, and offer support to help employees overcome challenges and achieve their goals.

Maintain a customer-centric focus

A strong sales culture is always customer-centric. This means that all decisions, strategies, and actions should be made with the customer's needs and desires in mind. To ensure the customer-centric focus is maintained, it is important to actively listen to customer feedback, adapt to market changes, and ensure the products and services offered meet the target audience's expectations.

Encourage innovation and creativity

Innovation and creativity are crucial to maintaining competitiveness and success in a constantly changing market. A successful sales culture should encourage employees to think creatively and propose new ideas and solutions to improve sales efficiency and effectiveness. This can be achieved by promoting an open and inclusive work environment where employees feel comfortable sharing their ideas and receiving feedback.

Regularly monitor and adjust the sales culture

Developing a strong sales culture is an ongoing and complex process that requires commitment, effort, and adaptability. It is essential to periodically evaluate the effectiveness of the sales culture and identify areas for improvement. This can be done by analyzing performance metrics, conducting internal surveys and employee feedback, and tracking industry trends.

Developing a sales culture in the company is a complex and ongoing process that requires commitment, effort, and adaptability. However, by following the steps described in this chapter and ensuring all employees are aligned with the company's values, goals, and expectations, it is possible to create a strong and successful sales culture that drives long-term growth and prosperity for the company.

Setting goals and objectives for the sales team

Well-defined objectives provide a sense of direction and purpose, help maintain the motivation and engagement of team members, and serve as a performance indicator to assess the success of sales strategies. In this chapter, we will cover the steps to establishing effective goals and targets for the sales team and how to ensure that these objectives are achieved.

Defining clear and specific objectives

The first step to establishing effective goals and targets is to clearly define what is expected to be achieved. This means being specific about what the sales team should accomplish, whether it is to increase revenue, improve customer retention, or expand market share. Specific objectives help the team understand exactly what is expected of them and develop effective strategies to achieve these goals.

Setting SMART goals

When setting goals for the sales team, it is important that they are SMART: **specific, measurable, attainable, relevant, and time-bound.** SMART goals ensure that the objectives are realistic, can be monitored and measured, and that the team has a clear understanding of the time needed to achieve them.

Aligning objectives with the overall company strategy

The goals and targets of the sales team should be aligned with the overall strategy and objectives of the company. This will ensure that the sales team works in synergy with other areas of the organization, creating a collaborative environment that drives overall business success.

Engaging the team in the goal-setting process

To ensure commitment and engagement from the sales team, it is important to involve them in the goal-setting process. This allows team members to provide feedback, share their concerns and suggestions, and feel responsible for the group's success. Involving the team in the goal-setting process also increases the likelihood that the goals are realistic and attainable.

Establishing individual and collective goals

It is critical to set individual and collective goals for the sales team. Individual goals ensure that each team member is responsible for their own performance, while collective goals promote collaboration and teamwork. In addition, balancing individual and collective goals can motivate team members to strive for their personal objectives as well as contribute to the overall success of the team.

Monitoring and Evaluating Progress Regularly

To ensure that the sales team is on track to achieve their goals and objectives, it is crucial to monitor and evaluate progress regularly. This can be done through weekly, monthly, or quarterly analyses, depending on the specific needs of the company and sales team. Monitoring progress allows for quickly identifying areas for improvement and adjusting sales strategies as needed.

Providing Constructive Feedback and Recognition

When evaluating the sales team's performance, it is important to provide constructive feedback and recognize the efforts of team members. This includes praising individual and collective achievements and identifying areas where improvements can be made. Constructive feedback and recognition help to maintain high morale and motivation, encouraging team members to continue striving to achieve their goals.

Adjusting Goals as Needed

Over time, market conditions, company goals, and sales team needs may change. Therefore, it is important to be flexible and adjust goals as needed. If a goal becomes irrelevant or unattainable, adjust it to reflect new circumstances and ensure that the sales team continues to work towards meaningful and achievable objectives.

Fostering a Culture of Continuous Learning

Encouraging the sales team to pursue personal and professional development is essential to maintaining motivation and continuously improving performance. This can include promoting training, workshops, and relevant events to enhance skills and knowledge, as well as creating a work environment that supports the exchange of ideas and experiences among team members.

Celebrating Success

When goals and objectives are achieved, it is important to celebrate the sales team's success. This can be done through celebration events, awards, and public recognition. Celebrating the sales team's success helps to reinforce the importance of working towards goals and maintaining high motivation levels.

Establishing effective goals and objectives for the sales team is crucial to ensuring long-term success for the department and the company as a whole.

By following the steps outlined in this chapter, you can create a productive and motivating work environment that encourages the sales team to reach their full potential and contribute **significantly to the overall success of the business.**

How to motivate the sales team for success

Motivating a sales team is essential to ensure its success. Motivation is the force that drives salespeople to achieve their goals, overcome challenges, and achieve outstanding performance. In this chapter, we will discuss several strategies to inspire and motivate your sales team towards success.

Open and transparent communication is the foundation of a motivated sales team. Encourage open dialogue between team members and leadership, and make sure everyone is aware of the company's goals and expectations. By maintaining open communication channels, you create a work environment where everyone feels supported and encouraged to give their best.

It is crucial to establish clear and achievable goals for the sales team. Goals should be specific, measurable, relevant, and time-bound, so salespeople know exactly what is expected of them and can track their progress. Celebrating achievements and milestones reached is an effective way to keep motivation high.

Empowering the team is another powerful strategy to increase motivation. When salespeople feel empowered and confident in their skills, they are more likely to take responsibility for their success and seek growth opportunities. Investing in the professional development of your sales team by offering training and resources can significantly contribute to increasing motivation and improving overall performance.

Recognition of performance and efforts of team members is essential to maintaining their motivation. Show appreciation for hard work and the achievements of each salesperson, whether through verbal praise, awards, or financial incentives. Creating a system of rewards and recognition can be an effective way to keep the sales team engaged and motivated.

Promoting a positive and collaborative work environment is also essential for sales team motivation. Encourage teamwork and collaboration, and help build strong relationships among team members. This creates an environment where salespeople feel supported and encouraged to achieve their goals.

Last but not least, it is essential to lead by example. An inspiring and motivated sales leader will have a significant impact on the motivation of their team. By demonstrating passion, energy, and enthusiasm in your work, you will convey this positive attitude to your team and inspire them to do their best.

Motivating the sales team towards success involves implementing various strategies, from open and transparent communication to investing in professional development and promoting a positive work environment. By putting these approaches into practice, you will create a motivated, committed, and successful sales team. Additionally, there are other actions you can take to keep your sales team motivated and committed to success.

Flexibility is an important aspect of sales team motivation. Allowing salespeople to have a certain degree of autonomy in decision-making and managing their time can increase job satisfaction and improve performance. Flexibility can also extend to working hours and remote work policies, helping team members balance their professional and personal responsibilities.

Establishing a shared sense of purpose is another powerful way to motivate your sales team. By clearly communicating the company's vision and mission, you help salespeople understand how their work contributes to the overall success of the organization. When sales team members feel connected to a higher purpose, they are more likely to commit and strive to achieve their goals.

Fostering healthy competition among team members can be an effective strategy to increase motivation. Competition, when conducted in a positive and constructive way, can encourage salespeople to push themselves to the limit and overcome their limits. To ensure that competitiveness does not become destructive, it is important to recognize the effort and performance of all team members and promote collaboration and mutual support.

Another way to motivate your sales team is to provide career advancement opportunities. Salespeople who see possibilities for growth and development within the company tend to feel more engaged and committed to their work. Establish a clear career plan for team members and encourage them to seek growth and promotion opportunities.

Another way to motivate your sales team is to provide career advancement opportunities. Salespeople who see possibilities for growth and development within the company tend to feel more engaged and committed to their work. Establish a clear career path for team members and encourage them to seek out growth and promotion opportunities.

Additionally, it is essential to pay attention to the emotional and mental well-being of your sales team. Sales work can be stressful and draining, and it is crucial to provide support and resources to help salespeople cope with work-related stress and pressure. This may include access to wellness and mental health programs, as well as creating a work environment that values work-life balance.

In summary, by combining all these strategies, you can create a work environment that inspires, motivates, and engages your sales team, leading to greater success and job satisfaction. Remember that motivation is a continuous process that requires constant effort and attention to ensure that your sales team continues to thrive and achieve excellent results.

How to deal with pressure and stress in sales

Dealing with pressure and stress is an inevitable part of professional life, especially in a highly competitive and results-oriented sales environment. However, it's crucial to learn how to effectively manage stress and pressure to ensure long-term success and well-being, both professionally and personally.

The first thing to understand is that stress is not necessarily a bad thing. A certain amount of stress can be beneficial, helping to maintain the motivation, energy, and focus necessary to achieve goals. However, when stress becomes excessive or chronic, it can have detrimental effects on physical and mental health, as well as work performance.

To effectively deal with pressure and stress in sales, it's important to adopt a multifaceted approach that includes time management, setting boundaries, developing healthy coping skills, and creating a balanced and supportive work environment.

Time management is an essential skill for dealing with pressure and stress in sales. This includes prioritizing tasks, setting realistic goals, and creating a balanced daily routine that allows for enough time for work and personal activities. By planning your day efficiently and productively, you can ensure that you're using your time in the best way possible and reduce the feeling of overwhelm and pressure.

Setting clear boundaries is another effective strategy for dealing with pressure and stress in sales. This can include boundaries related to work hours, availability expectations, and professional and personal responsibilities. By setting boundaries, you can create a healthier balance between work and personal life, which, in turn, can help reduce stress.

Developing healthy coping skills is crucial for dealing with pressure and stress in sales. This can include relaxation techniques such as meditation, deep breathing, and visualization exercises, as well as activities that help relieve stress, such as exercising, spending time with friends and family, or engaging in hobbies and leisure activities.

Finally, creating a balanced and supportive work environment can have a significant impact on the ability to deal with pressure and stress in sales. This can include encouraging teamwork and collaboration, promoting a culture of open and honest communication, and providing resources and support to help team members manage stress and pressure effectively.

Pressure and stress in sales are an inevitable part of the job, but adopting effective stress management strategies can help ensure long-term success and well-being.

Managing pressure and stress is an inevitable part of professional life, especially in a highly competitive and results-oriented sales environment. However, it is crucial to learn how to effectively manage stress and pressure to ensure long-term success and well-being, both professionally and personally.

The first thing to understand is that stress is not necessarily a bad thing. A certain amount of stress can be beneficial, helping to maintain the motivation, energy, and focus necessary to achieve goals. However, when stress becomes excessive or chronic, it can have harmful effects on physical and mental health, as well as job performance.

To effectively deal with pressure and stress in sales, it is important to adopt a multifaceted approach that includes time management, setting boundaries, developing healthy coping skills, and creating a balanced and supportive work environment.

Time management is an essential skill for dealing with pressure and stress in sales. This includes prioritizing tasks, setting realistic goals, and creating a balanced daily routine that allows for sufficient time for both work and personal activities. By planning your day efficiently and productively, you can ensure that you are using your time to the fullest and reduce the feeling of overwhelm and pressure.

Setting clear boundaries is another effective strategy for dealing with pressure and stress in sales. This can include boundaries related to work time, availability expectations, and professional and personal responsibilities. By setting boundaries, you can create a healthier balance between work and personal life, which, in turn, can help reduce stress.

Developing healthy coping skills is essential for dealing with pressure and stress in sales. This can include relaxation techniques, such as meditation, deep breathing, and visualization exercises, as well as activities that help relieve stress, such as exercising, spending time with friends and family, or engaging in hobbies and leisure activities.

Finally, creating a balanced and supportive work environment can have a significant impact on your ability to deal with pressure and stress in sales. This can include encouraging teamwork and collaboration, promoting a culture of open and honest communication, and providing resources and support to help team members manage stress and pressure effectively.

By managing time, setting boundaries, developing healthy coping skills, and creating a supportive work environment, you can create a resilient and successful sales team. It is also important to practice self-compassion and empathy towards yourself and your colleagues. Recognizing that pressure and stress are part of the process and that everyone has moments of difficulty can help build a more understanding and supportive environment.

Another useful strategy is to establish regular moments of relaxation and leisure with the team. This can include activities such as team lunches, celebrations of achievements, and events outside of the work environment. These moments help to create a bond between team members and provide opportunities to share experiences and talk about the difficulties faced at work.

It is also crucial to maintain a positive perspective and focus on the rewarding aspects of sales work. Celebrating small victories and recognizing the efforts of team members can have a significant impact on motivation and overall well-being. Additionally, encouraging a growth mindset can help the team approach challenges and stress in a more adaptable and resilient way.

Investing in training and professional development is also an effective way to reduce stress and pressure in sales. By providing opportunities for team members to improve their skills and knowledge, you can help them feel more confident and prepared to deal with the challenges of the job.

Finally, remember that self-care is essential for managing stress and pressure in sales. Ensuring that you and your team are taking care of your physical, mental, and emotional health is essential for maintaining a healthy and productive work environment.

In conclusion, dealing with pressure and stress in sales is an inevitable challenge, but by implementing these strategies and cultivating a supportive culture, it is possible to create a successful, resilient, and satisfied sales team.

The role of coaching in sales

Sales coaching is a powerful practice that can transform the performance of a sales team, leading to better and more consistent results. In this chapter, we will explore the role of sales coaching and how it can help create a winning sales team.

Coaching is a collaborative process in which an experienced coach works with a salesperson to help them develop skills, improve their performance, and achieve their sales goals. This process involves a combination of guidance, feedback, learning, and practice, allowing salespeople to overcome challenges and maximize their potential.

One of the main benefits of sales coaching is continuous improvement. By working regularly with a coach, salespeople have the opportunity to reflect on their performance, identify areas for improvement, and develop strategies to overcome obstacles. Coaching also helps create a culture of learning and development within the sales team, encouraging a constant pursuit of growth and improvement.

In addition, sales coaching can help develop communication and interpersonal skills of salespeople. These skills are crucial to creating meaningful connections with customers and closing sales successfully. The coach can assist salespeople in improving their ability to listen, ask effective questions, and adapt their sales approach to meet the needs and expectations of the customer.

Sales coaching can also have a significant impact on the motivation and commitment of salespeople. By receiving targeted support and guidance, salespeople feel more confident in their abilities and are encouraged to strive to achieve their goals. The coaching process also helps create accountability, ensuring that salespeople stay focused on their goals and the overall success of the team.

To successfully implement sales coaching, it is important to follow some recommended practices:

Select a qualified and experienced coach: An effective coach should have sales experience and knowledge of the latest techniques and strategies. They should also be excellent communicators and possess leadership and empathy skills.

Establish clear and measurable goals: Coaching goals should be specific, measurable, achievable, relevant, and time-limited (SMART). This will help ensure that the coaching process is focused and effective.

Create a trusting and supportive environment: Sales coaching can only be successful if salespeople feel comfortable sharing their challenges and concerns. Create an environment in which salespeople feel supported and encouraged to pursue growth and development.

Monitor progress and adjust as necessary: Sales coaching is an ongoing process that requires regular monitoring and adjustments. Make sure to track the progress of your salespeople and adjust your coaching strategies as necessary to ensure effective results.

In summary, sales coaching plays a crucial role in building a winning sales team. By investing in the development of skills, motivation, and performance of your salespeople, you are preparing your team to face market challenges and achieve exceptional results.

By incorporating sales coaching as an integral part of your company's sales strategy, you are contributing to the creation of a culture of continuous learning and development. This will not only help your sales team to stand out, but also ensure that the company as a whole is constantly evolving and adapting to market changes.

Finally, it is essential to remember that sales coaching is a long-term investment that will bring lasting benefits to your sales team and your company. Therefore, it is critical that you are committed to implementing and maintaining an effective coaching program, ensuring that your sales team can achieve their full potential and drive the success of the company.

Now that you understand the crucial role of sales coaching in building a winning sales team, it's time to start planning and implementing a coaching program that meets the specific needs of your team.

Remember that success in sales does not happen overnight, but through a continuous commitment to growth, development, and learning. With dedication and effort, you can create a high-performing sales team that will lead your company to success.

How to develop emotional intelligence in the sales team

Emotional intelligence (EI) is the ability to recognize, understand, and manage one's own emotions and the emotions of others. In the context of sales, EI is an essential skill for building strong relationships with clients, managing stress and pressure, and working effectively as a team.

The importance of emotional intelligence in sales

Emotional intelligence is a critical factor in sales success for several reasons:

Relationship building: The ability to understand and emotionally connect with clients is crucial for building trust and establishing lasting relationships.

Conflict resolution: Dealing with objections and conflicts is a common part of the sales process. EI helps salespeople stay calm and approach these situations in a productive manner.

Teamwork: Emotional intelligence is essential for effective collaboration within the sales team and between departments.

Stress management: EI enables salespeople to better handle the pressure and stress associated with sales work, improving their overall well-being and job performance.

Tips for developing emotional intelligence in the sales team

Self-awareness: Encourage team members to reflect on their own emotions and reactions in different sales situations. Self-awareness is the first step towards developing EI.

Empathy: Encourage salespeople to put themselves in the shoes of clients and consider their needs, concerns, and emotions. Empathy is the foundation for building strong relationships and generating trust.

Effective communication: Promote the importance of active listening and non-violent communication. This will help team members understand and express their own emotions and respond appropriately to clients' emotions.

Emotion management: Teach salespeople to recognize and control their emotions in high-pressure situations. Stress management techniques such as deep breathing, meditation, and scheduled breaks can be helpful.

Social skills development: Promote activities and training that help the team develop social skills such as teamwork, conflict resolution, and leadership.

Implementing an Emotional Intelligence Development Program

To develop emotional intelligence in your sales team, consider implementing a development program that includes the following components:

Assessment: Evaluate the current level of emotional intelligence of team members through questionnaires, interviews, or professional assessments.

Training: Invest in specific training and workshops for developing skills related to emotional intelligence, such as effective communication, empathy, and emotional management.

Feedback: Provide regular feedback to team members on their emotional skills and suggest areas for improvement. This may include coaching sessions, performance reviews, or group discussions.

Practice: Encourage salespeople to actively practice emotional intelligence skills in their daily work. This can be done through group exercises, role-playing, or simply paying more attention to their own emotions and those of others.

Monitoring and follow-up: Track the progress of team members in developing their emotional intelligence and celebrate improvements. If necessary, adjust the development program to meet individual needs and challenges.

Developing emotional intelligence in your sales team is critical to long-term success. By investing in the development of these skills, you will create a more resilient, collaborative, and effective team that can better connect with customers and generate superior results.

Emotional intelligence is a valuable skill that benefits not only professional but also personal life, contributing to overall well-being and job satisfaction for team members.

What is SPIN Selling and how to apply it

SPIN Selling is a sales methodology developed by Neil Rackham in his book "SPIN Selling," published in 1988. The acronym SPIN refers to a series of questions that salespeople should ask potential customers to identify their needs and present personalized solutions. The method is based on the following categories of questions: Situation, Problem, Implication, and Need for Solution.

This chapter will explore the SPIN Selling methodology in detail and provide guidance on how to apply it in your sales process to improve connection with customers and increase the chances of success.

Understanding SPIN Selling

SPIN Selling is a consultative sales method that focuses on understanding the customer's needs and presenting personalized solutions that solve their problems. The methodology consists of asking four types of questions:

Situation: These questions help to obtain basic information about the customer and their context. The goal is to understand the environment in which the customer operates and what challenges they may face.

Examples of situation questions:

What is the size of your company?

What are the main products or services you offer?

Who are your main competitors?

Problem: Problem questions aim to identify the difficulties and challenges faced by the customer. The salesperson should try to understand what problems the customer is trying to solve and how it affects their business.

Examples of problem questions:

What difficulties are you facing in your current operation?

Are you satisfied with the performance of your current product or service?

What kind of problems are your customers facing?

Implication: These questions explore the consequences of the identified problems, allowing the seller to demonstrate the urgency of resolving the issues and how it affects the customer.

Examples of implication questions:

How does this problem affect your profitability?

If this problem is not resolved, how will it impact your reputation in the market?

What are the possible long-term consequences if this situation persists?

Need for Solution: Solution need questions help the customer realize the importance of finding a solution to their problems and visualize how the seller's offer can be beneficial.

Examples of solution need questions:

What kind of solution do you think would be most effective in solving this problem?

If we could provide a solution that meets your needs, how would that benefit your company?

What is the value to you and your company if we can solve this problem?

Applying SPIN Selling to Your Sales Process

Now that you understand the SPIN Selling methodology, it's time to apply it to your sales process. Here are some steps to successfully implement SPIN Selling:

Preparation: Before entering a sales meeting, prepare by researching the customer and their business.

Ask open-ended questions: When starting the conversation with the customer, ask open-ended questions to stimulate discussion and facilitate identifying their needs. This will allow you to tailor your approach and offer a more personalized solution.

Listen actively: During the conversation, listen carefully to the customer and take note of relevant information. This will demonstrate respect and genuine interest, as well as help you better understand the customer's needs.

Adapt the SPIN approach: Depending on the customer's responses, adapt the sequence and focus of the SPIN questions to ensure you are addressing the most important issues and generating value.

Develop customized solutions: Based on the information gathered, develop customized solutions that address the identified problems and demonstrate how your offering can benefit the customer.

Present your solution: When presenting your solution, focus on the specific benefits it will bring to the customer. Use the information gathered during the conversation to emphasize how your solution directly addresses the customer's needs.

Overcome objections: Be prepared to face objections from the customer and use the information gathered during the conversation to provide convincing answers and solutions.

Closing: At the end of the conversation, work to obtain a commitment from the customer. This can be a sale, an agreement for a next meeting, or another action that moves the sales process forward.

Benefits of SPIN Selling

Implementing the SPIN Selling methodology into your sales process can bring several benefits, such as:

Better understanding of customer needs: By asking targeted questions, you can better understand the customer's needs and offer more personalized solutions.

Stronger customer relationships: SPIN Selling helps establish a deeper and more meaningful relationship with the customer, as it focuses on solving their problems, rather than just selling a product or service.

Increased sales and customer satisfaction: By offering solutions that meet the customer's needs, you will increase the chances of closing the sale and leaving the customer satisfied.

Improved communication skills: Practicing SPIN Selling improves your communication skills, allowing you to become a more efficient and persuasive salesperson.

The SPIN Selling methodology is a powerful approach that helps better understand customer needs and offer personalized solutions. Implementing this strategy into your sales process can lead to stronger customer relationships, increased sales, and improved communication skills.

How to use the BANT technique in sales

The BANT technique is one of the most well-known and widely used tools in sales for qualifying leads and identifying opportunities. Developed by IBM in the 1960s, the acronym BANT stands for the four essential criteria for determining if a lead is a good sales opportunity: Budget, Authority, Need, and Timeframe.

Understanding the BANT technique

The BANT technique is a method for qualifying leads based on four key criteria:

Budget: Does the customer have sufficient budget to acquire the offered product or service?

Authority: Does the person you are communicating with have the authority to make the purchasing decision, or do you need to involve other stakeholders?

Need: Is there a real and identifiable need for the product or service you offer?

Timeframe: What is the customer's timeframe for making a decision or implementing the solution?

By evaluating these criteria, you can determine if a lead is a viable sales opportunity and whether it's worth investing time and resources in the sales process.

How to apply the BANT technique in sales

To use the BANT technique in sales, follow these steps:

Ask specific questions: During your interactions with the customer, ask targeted questions to gather information about the four BANT criteria. For example, ask about available budget, decision-makers, specific needs, and desired timeframe for the solution.

Evaluate the responses: Analyze the customer's responses and determine if they meet the BANT criteria. If all conditions are met, the lead can be considered a viable sales opportunity.

Prioritize qualified leads: Identify leads that meet the BANT criteria and prioritize them in your sales pipeline, focusing your efforts on these potential customers.

Adapt your approach: Based on the information collected, adapt your sales approach to meet the specific needs and BANT criteria of the customer.

Track and adjust: Monitor the progress of your BANT-qualified leads and adjust your approach as necessary. This may include involving other stakeholders, presenting different budget options, or adapting your offer to better meet the customer's needs.

Benefits of using the BANT technique

The BANT technique offers several benefits for the sales team:

Improves sales efficiency: By focusing on BANT-qualified leads, your sales team can direct their efforts towards opportunities with a higher likelihood of conversion, improving the efficiency of the sales process.

Increases conversion rates: The BANT technique helps to identify leads with a higher probability of becoming customers, which can lead to a higher conversion rate.

Improves communication with the customer: By asking targeted questions and collecting important information about the customer, your sales team can develop a deeper understanding of the customer's needs and personalize the sales approach accordingly.

Facilitates sales forecasting: By utilizing the BANT technique, your sales team can more accurately predict sales opportunities and better estimate future results.

Reduces the sales cycle: By focusing on qualified leads and eliminating those that do not meet the BANT criteria, your sales team can reduce time spent on less promising leads and shorten the sales cycle.

Aids in product and service development: The BANT technique provides valuable information about customer needs, helping your company identify areas for improvement and opportunities to develop new products and services.

The BANT technique is a valuable tool for qualifying leads and maximizing the effectiveness of your sales team. By applying the

BANT technique in sales, you can identify the best sales opportunities, enhance your sales approach, and increase conversion rates. By adopting this strategy, your company will be on the path to implementing a winning sales department.

How to use the GPCT model to generate sales

The GPCT model is a powerful technique that helps sales teams to identify and understand customer needs more effectively. The GPCT acronym stands for Goals, Plans, Challenges, and Timeline. In this chapter, we will cover each element of the GPCT model and how to apply them to drive sales.

The first step in using the GPCT model is to identify the customer's goals. Understanding the customer's goals allows salespeople to demonstrate how their products or services can help them achieve them. During conversations with customers, salespeople should ask specific questions to uncover their goals and understand how they relate to their business needs.

Next, it's important to explore the plans that customers already have in place to achieve these goals. This step involves investigating what strategies and resources customers are currently using and how your company can complement or enhance these efforts. By showing that your solution fits into the customer's existing plans, salespeople increase the chances of closing the sale.

The challenges that customers face are also a critical component of the GPCT model. By identifying the obstacles that prevent customers from reaching their goals, salespeople can position their products or services as solutions to overcome these challenges. To do this, salespeople should ask questions that help reveal the challenges and understand how their offering can help solve them.

Finally, the timeline is an essential part of the GPCT model. Understanding the customer's timeline allows salespeople to tailor their proposals and deliveries according to the customer's expectations. In addition, understanding the timeline helps the sales team prioritize opportunities according to the urgency and potential for closing sales.

By applying the GPCT model, salespeople can create a more personalized and effective sales approach, focusing on the specific goals, plans, challenges, and timelines of customers. This customer-centric approach facilitates the development of stronger and more lasting relationships, increasing customer satisfaction and loyalty.

In conclusion, the GPCT model is a valuable tool for driving sales, allowing salespeople to better understand customer needs and expectations. By using the GPCT model in their interactions with customers, your sales team will be better prepared to present solutions that align with customer goals and challenges, thus improving the likelihood of successful sales and implementing a winning sales department.

Strategies for dealing with customers at different stages of the sales funnel

The success of a sales department depends on its ability to understand and meet the needs of customers at each stage of the sales funnel. In this chapter, we will cover effective strategies for dealing with customers at different stages of the sales funnel, from awareness to closing the sale.

Awareness

In the awareness stage, customers are starting to realize they have a problem or need. It is essential for the sales team to focus on attracting the attention of these potential customers by providing educational and informative content that helps them identify their needs and understand how your company can help.

Strategies for this stage include:

Creating relevant and educational content such as blogs, e-books, and videos;

Participating in forums and discussion groups where potential customers may be looking for information;

Using social media and targeted advertising to attract the attention of potential customers;

Establishing partnerships with influencers or industry thought leaders to increase brand visibility.

Consideration

In the consideration stage, customers have identified the problem and are researching solutions. The goal of the sales team in this stage is to show potential customers that your company is the best option to solve their needs.

Strategies for this stage include:

Providing advanced and detailed resources and case studies that demonstrate the value of your solution;

Promoting events such as workshops or live demonstrations where potential customers can experience your solution first-hand;

Implementing email marketing campaigns to nurture leads and keep them engaged with the brand;

Using testimonials and references from satisfied customers to build trust and credibility.

Decision

In the decision stage, customers are ready to make a decision and choose the solution that best meets their needs. The goal of the sales team in this stage is to overcome objections and close the sale.

Strategies for this stage include:

Providing personalized proposals that address the specific needs and goals of the customer;

Offering incentives or discounts to encourage quick decision making;

Conducting sales meetings or calls to address concerns and answer questions in real-time;

Establishing an efficient follow-up process to ensure potential customers do not go unanswered during the decision-making process.

Post-sale

After the sale, it is essential to continue nurturing the relationship with the customer and ensuring their satisfaction. A satisfied customer will not only provide valuable referrals but may also become a repeat customer.

Strategies for this stage include:

Providing high-quality customer support to resolve issues and promptly answer questions;

Offering additional training and resources to help customers get the most out of the solution purchased;

Maintaining regular contact with customers through email, phone, or in-person visits to ensure their needs are being met and to identify upsell or cross-sell opportunities;

Soliciting feedback from customers and implementing improvements based on their suggestions and needs.

By understanding and addressing the needs of customers at each stage of the sales funnel, the sales team will be well-positioned to build strong and lasting relationships with customers and, consequently, increase sales and the success of the department.

To deal with customers at different stages of the sales funnel, it is crucial to adapt your approach and strategy based on the specific needs and challenges of each stage. By doing so, the sales team can ensure a more personalized and effective experience for the customer, which in turn leads to greater sales success and customer satisfaction.

How to develop empathy in sales

Empathy is an essential skill for sales professionals as it allows them to truly connect with customers and understand their needs and concerns. Developing empathy in sales is an effective way to create strong and lasting relationships, which can lead to increased sales and customer satisfaction.

Firstly, it's important to understand that empathy is not just an innate skill but also something that can be learned and developed over time. To start, salespeople should focus on actively listening to customers. This means giving full attention to what the customer is saying without interruptions and asking questions to deepen the understanding of their concerns and needs.

Another important tip for developing empathy in sales is to put oneself in the customer's shoes. This involves imagining what it would be like to be in the customer's position and how they would feel facing the concerns and challenges they are experiencing. This perspective can help the sales team better understand the customer's needs and offer more effective solutions.

Additionally, empathy in sales can be enhanced by working on emotional communication. This means being able to express and recognize emotions, both one's own and those of customers. By understanding and validating the customer's emotions, salespeople can establish a deeper and more authentic connection, which can lead to greater trust and customer satisfaction.

It's equally important to be genuine and transparent when dealing with customers. Salespeople should avoid using manipulative or dishonest tactics as this can harm trust and empathy. Instead, it's better to be honest and open about the product or service's capabilities, as well as realistic timelines and expectations.

Lastly, developing empathy in sales requires practice and time. Salespeople should strive to incorporate empathy into all customer interactions and seek feedback to further improve their skills. By doing so, the sales team can create stronger and more lasting relationships with customers, ultimately leading to greater sales success.

As part of the process of developing empathy in sales, it's essential that sales professionals also invest in their own personal development. This includes working on emotional intelligence, communication skills, and the ability to manage stress. By developing these skills, salespeople will be better equipped to handle the different situations that may arise during customer interactions.

Customer feedback is a valuable tool for improving empathy in sales. Encourage team members to seek feedback from customers after interactions, especially if they feel that the emotional connection could have been stronger. Learning from customer experiences and making adjustments to sales approaches can help the team become more empathetic and successful.

Additionally, it's crucial to create a work environment that encourages and supports the development of empathy. This includes offering training and resources for team members, as well as creating an organizational culture that values empathy and customer connection. Encourage team members to share their experiences and learnings with each other, as this can reinforce the importance of empathy in the sales process.

Another way to develop empathy in sales is through analyzing success stories. Studying examples of successful customer interactions and identifying the key elements that led to these positive results can provide valuable insights for the sales team. By analyzing these cases, salespeople can identify areas where empathy was a critical factor for success and apply these lessons to their own customer interactions.

Lastly, it's important to remember that developing empathy in sales is a continuous process. Salespeople should always be on the lookout for opportunities to improve their skills and learn from customer and coworker feedback. By doing so, the sales team will constantly be improving their ability to connect with customers and understand their needs, ultimately leading to greater sales success.

Developing empathy in sales is a crucial skill for sales professionals as it allows them to create deeper and more meaningful connections with customers. Through active listening, emotional communication, personal development, and continuous learning, the sales team can enhance their ability to be empathetic and, in turn, increase customer satisfaction and sales success.

By investing in the development of empathy, the sales team will be prepared to tackle sales challenges and build long-lasting and successful relationships with customers.

Techniques for dealing with difficult customers

Dealing with difficult customers is an inevitable part of sales work. However, facing these challenges with patience, skill, and empathy can turn a challenging situation into an opportunity for growth and success.

Stay calm and control your emotions

The first and most important rule when dealing with difficult customers is to stay calm and control your emotions. Take a deep breath and remember that your main goal is to solve the customer's problem and ensure their satisfaction. Avoid taking criticism and complaints personally and focus on listening carefully and responding professionally and objectively.

Listen attentively

Active listening is an essential skill for dealing with difficult customers. Pay attention to what the customer is saying, ask questions to clarify their concerns, and demonstrate empathy for their situation. By listening carefully, you can identify the root cause of the problem and begin working on a solution.

Validate the customer's feelings

Validating the customer's feelings is an effective technique for establishing rapport and creating an emotional connection. Acknowledge the customer's emotions and show that you understand their frustration. For example, you can say: "I understand that you are upset about the situation. I would feel the same way if I were in your shoes."

Be empathetic and offer solutions

After listening and validating the customer's feelings, offer practical solutions to resolve the problem. Show empathy and work together with the customer to find a resolution that satisfies both parties. Remember that the main goal is to ensure customer satisfaction and maintain a healthy and lasting relationship.

Establish boundaries and maintain a professional stance

While it is important to be empathetic and understanding, it is also crucial to establish boundaries and maintain a professional stance. If a customer becomes abusive or demands impossible solutions, do not hesitate to set boundaries and communicate your expectations clearly and firmly. Remember that you deserve respect and that maintaining a professional stance is fundamental to success in sales.

Learn from experience

Each interaction with a difficult customer is an opportunity for learning and growth. Analyze the situation and identify areas where you can improve your communication, empathy, and problem-solving skills. Share your experiences with team members and discuss strategies for dealing with difficult customers in the future.

Be flexible and adaptable

When dealing with difficult customers, it's important to be flexible and adaptable in your approach. Each customer is unique and may require a different strategy for resolving their problems and calming their frustrations. Be willing to adjust your communication style and approach to meet the customer's specific needs.

Ask for feedback

Asking for feedback from customers, even difficult ones, is an excellent way to improve your sales performance. Ask the customer to share their perceptions about the interaction and what could have been done differently. This information is valuable for your personal and professional growth, as well as for improving the company's sales approach.

Follow up and stay in touch

After resolving a situation with a difficult customer, don't forget to follow up and stay in touch. This shows the customer that you care about their ongoing satisfaction and are willing to do whatever it takes to ensure that they remain satisfied. Follow-up also provides an opportunity to strengthen the relationship and increase the chances of future sales.

Invest in training and development

Last but not least, invest in training and development to improve your skills in dealing with difficult customers. Attend courses, workshops, and seminars on communication, conflict resolution, and empathy. Learning from experts and fellow professionals is a great way to expand your skills and increase your effectiveness in dealing with difficult customers.

By applying these techniques and investing in your professional development, you'll be better prepared to face the challenges that difficult customers present and turn these situations into opportunities for growth and success. Remember that the ultimate goal is to ensure customer satisfaction and build lasting relationships that benefit both the customer and your company.

How to use storytelling in sales

Storytelling in sales is a powerful art that can help capture customers' attention, establish emotional connections, and ultimately lead to successful sales. Stories have the power to transport and engage us, and when used effectively, can be a persuasive and convincing tool in sales.

First and foremost, it is important to understand what storytelling is. Essentially, storytelling is the art of telling structured and engaging stories. In sales, this means using stories to illustrate the benefits of your product or service, overcome objections, and create an emotional connection with the customer.

To start using storytelling in sales, follow these steps:

Know your audience

To create engaging stories that resonate with your customers, it is essential to understand who they are, what their needs and desires are, and what motivates them. Ask questions and listen carefully to the answers to gain valuable insights that will help shape your stories.

Identify the problem

An effective sales story starts with identifying a problem that your customer is facing. This problem should be something that your product or service can solve. By starting your story with the problem, you establish common ground and create a sense of urgency.

Describe the solution

After identifying the problem, present the solution that your product or service offers. Show how the solution fits the customer's needs and desires and how it can improve their life. Use examples and vivid details to help the customer visualize the results that can be achieved.

Share success stories

Success stories from previous customers are a great way to show how your product or service has worked in the past. Share these stories to create credibility and help the customer imagine how their own life can be improved with the solution you are offering.

Engage the customer in the story

Incorporate the customer into your story by asking questions and involving them in the narrative. This will help them emotionally connect with the story and feel more invested in the solution. Additionally, hearing the customer's perspective can provide valuable insights that can be used to adjust your approach and improve your chances of closing the sale.

Practice and refine

Practice makes perfect, and the same goes for storytelling in sales. Practice telling your stories multiple times to ensure a smooth and engaging delivery. Seek feedback from colleagues and supervisors and adjust your approach as needed.

By mastering the art of storytelling in sales, you can create an emotional connection with your customers, overcome objections, and ultimately increase your chances of closing successful deals. Here are some additional tips for improving your storytelling skills:

Focus on quality, not quantity

Don't overwhelm your customers with too many stories. Instead, choose one or two high-impact stories that are relevant to the customer's problem and demonstrate the benefits of your product or service.

Use simple, straightforward language

When telling a story, avoid technical jargon and use clear, straightforward language that is easy to understand. This will help ensure that your message is understood and remembered.

Be authentic

The most effective stories are those that come from the heart. Be sincere and genuine when sharing your stories, and your customers will notice your authenticity.

Study great storytellers

Learn from the best by observing and studying great storytellers. This may include motivational speakers, comedians, authors, and other sales professionals. Observe how they structure their stories, engage the audience, and use language to create an emotional impact.

Adapt to the customer's needs

Each customer is unique, and your stories should be tailored to meet the specific needs and interests of each individual. Pay attention to the verbal and nonverbal cues that your customers provide and adjust your storytelling approach as needed.

Learn from your mistakes

Not every story will be successful, and that's okay. Learn from your mistakes and use that feedback to improve your stories and future approaches.

Storytelling is an essential skill for any sales professional. By learning how to tell engaging and emotionally impactful stories, you can create deeper connections with your customers, overcome objections, and drive your sales. Practice and refine your storytelling skills, and see how this powerful tool can transform your sales approach and lead to greater success.

How to use gamification to sell more

Gamification is a technique that uses game elements and mechanics to motivate and engage people in activities that are not related to games. In the world of sales, gamification can be used to motivate the team, increase productivity, and ultimately sell more. In this article, we will explore how to apply gamification to improve the performance of your sales team and achieve incredible results.

Gamification works because it taps into people's competitive nature and their desire to improve. By incorporating game elements such as points, levels, challenges, and rewards, you can motivate your sales team to work harder and have fun while doing it.

An effective way to implement gamification in your sales team is to establish clear goals and challenges. For example, you can create a points system where team members earn points for achieving sales goals, closing deals, or completing specific tasks. These points can be accumulated and exchanged for rewards such as prizes, days off, or other perks.

Another approach is to create healthy competition among team members. You can establish monthly or quarterly goals and reward the salespeople who achieve or exceed those goals. This not only promotes a spirit of collaboration but also encourages team members to challenge themselves and strive for continuous improvement.

Gamification can also be used to encourage skill development and continuous learning. For example, you can create a level system where team members can level up by completing training courses or attending workshops. This not only helps to improve the sales skills of team members but also demonstrates your commitment to growth and professional development.

To ensure that gamification is effective, it is crucial to establish a monitoring and feedback system. Track team members' progress towards established goals and challenges and provide regular feedback on their performance. This will help to maintain motivation and engagement among team members, allowing them to see how their actions are affecting results.

Gamification should also be flexible and adaptable to changes in the needs of the team and the market. Be open to adjusting your approaches and goals as necessary and listen to team members' feedback to ensure that gamification remains an effective motivator.

It is essential to use gamification ethically and responsibly. Avoid creating an overly competitive work environment or pressuring team members to achieve unattainable goals. Gamification should be used as a tool to inspire and motivate, not to punish or create a toxic work environment.

Gamification can be a powerful tool to help your sales team achieve success and improve performance. By incorporating game elements such as goals, challenges, rewards, and competitions, you can create a fun, engaging, and motivating work environment for your team.

Remember to consider the culture and specific needs of your team when implementing gamification. Each team is unique and may require different approaches to achieve the best results. Be flexible and willing to adjust your strategy as necessary to ensure that gamification remains effective and beneficial.

Additionally, it is important to communicate the rules and expectations of gamification clearly to the entire team. This will help to ensure that everyone understands the purpose and benefits of the system and how it works. Transparency and open communication are essential to ensure that gamification is successful and adopted by all team members.

By using gamification effectively and responsibly, you can help your sales team reach new levels of success. Over time, you will notice an increase in productivity, job satisfaction, and sales results, leading to a truly winning sales department.

How to maintain continuous improvement in the sales department and adapt to market changes

In the business world, change is the only constant. To ensure the continuous success of your sales department, it's essential to always be evolving and adapting to changes in the market. Here are some tips to help maintain the continuous evolution of your sales department and adapt to changes in the market.

Stay aware of industry trends and changes: Stay updated on news, trends, and technological advances in your industry. Attend industry events, seminars, and conferences to stay informed and connect with other sales professionals. This will help you identify potential opportunities and threats and adjust your sales approach accordingly.

Invest in training and development: Provide your sales team with continuous training and professional development opportunities. This will help them improve their skills, learn new techniques, and adapt to changes in the market. Foster a culture of learning, encouraging the team to share their experiences and knowledge with each other.

Monitor performance and results: Establish clear and measurable goals for your sales team and regularly monitor progress towards these goals. Analyze data to identify trends and areas for improvement. This will allow you to make quick and proactive adjustments to your sales strategy as needed.

Be agile and flexible: As the market changes, you may need to adjust your sales approach and tactics. Be willing to try new ideas and approaches and abandon those that are no longer working. Adopting an agile and flexible mindset will allow you to quickly adapt to changes and keep your sales team on track.

Cultivate innovation: Encourage your sales team to think outside the box and propose new ideas to improve sales and customer service. Allow room for experimentation and creativity, and reward those who present innovative solutions to the challenges faced by the department.

Maintain open communication: Promote a work environment where communication is valued and encouraged. Encourage your sales team to share their opinions, concerns, and ideas. This will help to quickly identify problems and opportunities for improvement, allowing you to make real-time adjustments and continue evolving.

Adapt to changes in consumer behavior: With the advancement of technology and social media, consumer behavior is constantly changing. Understand the needs and expectations of your customers and adjust your sales approach to effectively meet them. This may include the use of new communication channels, personalized offers, or the adoption of new engagement strategies.

Use technology to your advantage: Implement sales tools and software that can help automate processes, improve communication, and provide valuable information on sales performance and trends. This will help increase the department's efficiency and allow you to make more informed, data-driven decisions.

Collaborate with other departments: Work together with other departments in the company, such as marketing, product, and customer support, to create an integrated and coordinated approach to sales. This will help ensure that you are providing a consistent and high-quality experience for your customers at all touchpoints.

Promote resilience: Change can be difficult and stressful for team members. Help promote resilience by encouraging effective stress management and work-life balance. This will allow your sales team to remain motivated and committed, even in times of change and uncertainty.

Continuously evaluate and refine: Regularly assess your sales strategy and department performance to identify areas for improvement and growth opportunities. Be willing to adjust your approach and experiment with new strategies to continue evolving and adapting to changes in the market.

By following these tips, you can ensure that your sales department continues to evolve and adapt to changes in the market. This will not only help maintain the success of your team, but also ensure that your company remains competitive and relevant in the constantly changing business landscape.

Conclusion

In conclusion, throughout this book, we have explored the fundamental elements for creating and managing a winning sales department. We have covered a variety of strategies, techniques, and best practices that, when applied properly, have the potential to drive sales performance and increase customer satisfaction.

Based on all the chapters, it is clear that success in sales is not the result of a single factor. Instead, it is the result of a combination of various practices and approaches, from the use of modern tools and technologies to building solid, long-lasting relationships with customers. Each element of the sales department needs to be carefully managed and adapted to the specific needs of your company and your target audience.

A winning sales department is one that can adapt to changes in the market and evolve continuously. Therefore, it is crucial that sales leaders are always open to learning, exploring new approaches, and investing in the continuous development of their teams.

By implementing the strategies and techniques presented in this book, you will be taking an important step towards creating a winning sales department. However, remember that success is a continuous process, requiring effort, dedication, and commitment from the entire team.

By staying up-to-date on market trends and continuing to invest in improving your team's skills, you will be ensuring a future of success and continuous growth for your sales department and your company.

If you have made it this far, thank you for joining me on this journey, and I sincerely hope that all the valuable lessons taught here can help you create and maintain a winning sales department.

I wish you and your team all the success and prosperity in your future sales endeavors.

Joelmir Carvalho

References

ALDRICH, H.; HERKER, D. Boundary spanning roles and organization structure. Academy of Management Review, v. 2, n. 2, p. 217-230, 1977.

CHALL, J.; SPINELLI, S. SPIN Selling: Situation Problem Implication Need-Payoff. New York: McGraw-Hill, 1988.

CONGER, J. A.; KANUNGO, R. N. Charismatic leadership in organizations. Thousand Oaks: Sage Publications, 1998.

GARTNER. Magic Quadrant for Sales Force Automation. Disponível em: https://www.gartner.com/en/documents/3986305/magic-quadrant-for-sales-force-automation. Acesso em: 20 mar. 2023.

GITOMER, J. The Little Red Book of Selling: 12.5 Principles of Sales Greatness. Austin: Bard Press, 2004.

GLOVER, J. The BANT Sales Qualification Method: The Ultimate Guide. Disponível em: https://www.jillkonrath.com/sales-blog/bant-sales-qualification-method. Acesso em: 20 mar. 2023.

GOLDENBERG, B. CRM in Real Time: Empowering Customer Relationships. Medford: Information Today, Inc., 2008.

HOPKINS, T.; SMITH, D. Mastering the Complex Sale: How to Compete and Win When the Stakes are High! Hoboken: John Wiley & Sons, 2010.

KAPLAN, R. S.; NORTON, D. P. The Balanced Scorecard: Translating Strategy into Action. Boston: Harvard Business School Press, 1996.

KOTLER, P.; KELLER, K. L. Marketing Management. 15. ed. Upper Saddle River: Prentice Hall, 2016.

NUTSHELL. The Complete Guide to GPCT: A Goal-Oriented Sales Approach. Disponível em: https://www.nutshell.com/blog/complete-guide-to-gpct/. Acesso em: 20 mar. 2023.

PINK, D. H. Drive: The Surprising Truth About What Motivates Us. New York: Riverhead Books, 2011.

RAINS, M. Using SWOT Analysis in Business Planning. Disponível em: https://www.businessknowhow.com/strategy/swot.htm. Acesso em: 20 mar. 2023.

RAVEN, B. H.; KRIEGER, R. M. Dyadic Interaction: An Exchange of Information Leading to Increased Understanding of the Other. In: ADLER, L. L.; TOWNE, L. (Orgs.). The Practice of Interpersonal Communication. New York: Prentice-Hall, 1970.

ROGERS, S.; LAFORGE, R. W. Entrepreneurial selling: The BARREL Model of sales training. Journal of Personal Selling and Sales Management, v. 20, n. 2, p. 125-136, 2000.

TREACY, M.; WIERSEMA, F. The Discipline of Market Leaders: Choose Your Customers, Narrow Your Focus, Dominate Your Market. Reading: Addison-Wesley, 1995.

VAYNERCHUK, G. Jab, Jab, Jab, Right Hook: How to Tell Your Story in a Noisy Social World. New York: HarperCollins Publishers, 2013.

WEINBERG, G. M. The Psychology of Computer Programming. New York: Van Nostrand Rein

ZIGLAR, Z. Secrets of Closing the Sale. New York: Berkley Books, 1984.

ZOLTNERS, A. A.; SINHA, P.; LORIMER, S. E. Building a Winning Sales Management Team: The Force Behind the Sales Force. Evanston: ZS Associates, 2011.

ZWILLING, M. 10 Steps for Entrepreneurs to Master Emotional Intelligence. Disponível em: https://www.forbes.com/sites/martinzwilling/2013/12/15/10-steps-for-entrepreneurs-to-master-emotional-intelligence/. Acesso em: 20 mar. 2023.

www.ingramcontent.com/pod-product-compliance
Lightning Source LLC
Chambersburg PA
CBHW071134220526
45467CB00015B/975